K-Pop Fandom

K-Pop Fandom

Performing *Deokhu* from the 1990s to Today

Areum Jeong

University of Michigan Press

Ann Arbor

Published in the United States of America by the
University of Michigan Press
First published January 2026

A CIP catalog record for this book is available from the British Library.

Library of Congress Cataloging-in-Publication Data

Names: Jeong, Areum author | Michigan Publishing (University of Michigan) publisher
Title: K-Pop fandom : performing Deokhu from the 1990s to today / Areum Jeong.
Other titles: Performing Deokhu from the 1990s to today
Description: Ann Arbor [Michigan] : University of Michigan Press, 2026. | Includes bibliographical references (pages 147–156) and index.
Identifiers: LCCN 2025038055 (print) | LCCN 2025038056 (ebook) | ISBN 9780472077892 hardcover | ISBN 9780472057894 paperback | ISBN 9780472905652 ebook other
Subjects: LCSH: Popular music—Social aspects—Korea (South) | K-pop (Subculture) | Music fans—Korea (South)
Classification: LCC ML3917.K6 J46 2026 (print) | LCC ML3917.K6 (ebook) | DDC 782.4216/3095195—dc23/eng/20251113
LC record available at https://lccn.loc.gov/2025038055
LC ebook record available at https://lccn.loc.gov/2025038056

DOI: https://doi.org/10.3998/mpub.12903806

This publication was supported by the 2024 Korean Studies Grant Program of the Academy of Korean Studies (AKS-2024-P003).

The University of Michigan Press's open access publishing program is made possible thanks to additional funding from the University of Michigan Office of the Provost and the generous support of contributing libraries.

Cover photograph © Areum Jeong

Authorized Representative: Easy Access System Europe, Mustamäe tee 50, 10621 Tallinn, Estonia, gpsr.requests@easproject.com

To G1, my first oppa,
who inspired me to begin this project,
and
To Taeyong, my forever friend,
who gave me the strength to finish writing.

Contents

Digital materials related to this title can be found on the Fulcrum platform via the following citable URL: https://doi.org/10.3998/mpub.12903806

Illustrations

Acknowledgments

First and foremost, this book is for all of the K-pop fans out there. Thank you for inspiring this project, being part of it, agreeing to be interviewed, and sharing your stories and innermost thoughts. I learn so much from you every day.

I am grateful to the scholars who have offered comments and feedback on earlier drafts of the research at conferences and meetings that took place at the American Society for Theatre Research, Fan Studies Network North America, Pop Conference, Society for Cinema and Media Studies, the K-pop Beyond BTS: Media Technology, Creative Industries, and Fandom Culture Seminar, Ewha-Exeter Symposium at Ewha W. University, K-pop and the West: Media, Fandom, and Transnational Politics Symposium at University at Buffalo, State University of New York, Reputation Symposium at Oxford University, and the K-Pop: Musical Production and Consumption Conference at Yale University. I have learned so much from our discussions.

The Academy of Korean Studies and the American Society for Theatre Research supported this project, helping me to travel and publish.

Robert Morris University provided time and space to write the book. I will always cherish my time at the Rooney House and would like to thank Sushil Acharya, Jennifer Creamer, and Anthony Moretti for their warm hospitality and support.

I am grateful for my wonderful colleagues and students at Arizona State University, especially Dean Jeffrey Cohen, Dean Kenro Kusumi, Director Michael Tueller, Interim Director Sara Beaudrie, and my mentors Sookja Cho, Markus Cruse, Ana Hedberg Olenina, Robert Tuck, and Daniel Gilfillan. Thank you for your strong leadership and support.

Special thanks to Jena Gaines and Shanon Fitzpatrick, who read every word of this project, and Laura Portwood-Stacer, who demystified the book proposal writing process. I could not have done this without your thorough editing and feedback. I would also like to express my gratitude to Sara Jo Cohen, Annie Carter, Haley Winkle, Juliette Snyder, Danielle Coty-Fattal, Sarah Berg, and Mary Hashman at the University of Michigan Press for believing in and supporting this project.

This project began after I finished my doctoral dissertation, and I am grateful to the friends and mentors who cheered me from the early stages of research and writing, especially Thomas Baudinette, Mathieu Berbiguier, Julie Choi, Stephanie Choi, Ga Young Chung, Jongyeon Joy Ee, Jenna Gibson, Tamar Herman, Samantha James, Eunkyo Kang, Hieyoon Kim, and So-Rim Lee.

I would like to thank my parents, Dongyoul Jeong and Hosoon Kim, for patiently enduring a daughter obsessed with K-pop all her life.

Last but not least, I would like to thank G1, my first *oppa*, who inspired me to begin this project, and Taeyong, my forever friend, who gave me the strength to finish writing. I love you.

Introduction

According to statistics released by the Korea Foundation, there are more than 200 million fans of Korean pop culture around the globe. The K-pop group BTS, one of the most popular musical acts in the world, calls their fandom "ARMY," a fitting moniker for the powerful role fans have played in propelling their success. Highly organized and complexly networked, K-pop fandom is a community that mobilizes its resources, especially digital media and technology, to set and achieve communal goals. Today, everything from the careers of individual idols to the fate of an entire multinational industry relies on the labor that K-pop fans perform in service to the music, entertainment, and entertainers they love.

Since K-pop's origins in the late twentieth century, fan practices have been central to its production as an artistic and cultural phenomenon and behemoth global industry. Even as the music and industry have evolved, fans of K-pop have found happiness, encouragement, and a sense of community through the special connections they forge with K-pop stars and the broader fan base. Meanwhile, K-pop's success in Korea and around the world would not have been possible without the creative contributions of an enthusiastic, diverse, and seemingly ever-growing fandom. From promoting specific idols and groups to generating enthusiasm for the industry more broadly, fans massively influence the business of K-pop and its cultural and social significance.

And yet, even as fans have by now been widely recognized as important to the spectacular phenomenon that is K-pop, we are far from a systematic understanding of fan practices as *labor* practices—that is, as work that produces value and without which K-pop as we know it would not exist. In part, this is because of the ageist and sexist presumptions that structure whose activities count as "labor" and which realms of human cultural, social, and economic activity are typically seen as realms of "production." It is also, I think, the result of the ways that K-pop fandom and its practices have changed over time. As a hardcore K-pop fan since the early 1990s, I have witnessed vast transformations in K-pop fandom, fan identity, and the roles fans perform to shape and promote the industry. Over the past three decades, fan labor has expanded, intensified, and diversified along myriad dimensions, assuming novel social, technological, and economic forms, some of which are unique to K-pop, and some of which reflect broader cultural and industrial logics of globalized mass entertainment culture.

K-Pop Fandom: Performing Deokhu from the 1990s to Today is a study of K-pop that centers fans and their labor. Rather than framing fans primarily as consumers of K-pop, it insists that fan practices and activities constitute a central productive force, shaping not only K-pop's explosive global popularity but also K-pop's cultural and social impacts, cultural politics, and horizons of possibility. In particular, this book argues that K-pop fans, in performing *deokhu*—a Korean term connoting an "avid fan"—perform a kind of *materialization of affective labor*. This materialization of affective labor takes place across diverse fandom arenas and processes, from generalized, collective, and communal fan activities to decentralized, personalized labor that represents individual fans' personalities and performances of care.[1]

Affective labor, as scholars have theorized, refers to the kinds of work that produces, maintains, and manages emotions, feelings, and experiences, including the kinds of intensely felt individual and collective experiences of enjoyment and belonging K-pop elicits in its legions of fans worldwide. In Marxian economics, the "labor process" describes how labor is transformed into tangible goods that have value. In a more recent theoretical discussion, Michael Hardt and Antonio Negri focus on the role affective labor plays in postmodern production:

> Affective labor . . . is labor that produces or manipulates affects. . . . One can recognize affective labor, for example, in the work of legal assistants, flight attendants, and fast food workers (service with a smile). One indication of the rising importance of affective labor, at least in the dominant countries, is the tendency for employers to highlight education, attitude, character, and "prosocial" behavior as the primary skills employees need. A worker with a good attitude and social skills is another way of saying a worker is adept at affective labor.[2]

Affective labor is work carried out that is intended to produce or modify emotional experiences in people, and it takes place in both formal work environments as well as realms of everyday life. Building upon Marxist labor discourse, Sara Ahmed describes emotions as a form of capital; she states that "affect does not reside positively in the sign or commodity, but is produced as an effect of its circulation."[3] Here, we might stop to note that the circulation of commodities, including K-pop, does not happen on its own. Rather, it often depends on acts of consumption but also processes of promoting and sharing—work that may be primarily performed by fans. Not coincidentally, affective labor is often performed by women and other less-empowered or minoritized groups in society. And in addition to its underrepresentation in popular and academic conceptualizations of labor, it is not uncommon for it to be under- or un-compensated. Scholars in media studies such as Mel Stanfill and Megan Condis emphasize that recognizing and valuing fan activities as labor is important; they explain that examining fan activities via the labor framework values what fans are doing, while the pleasure framework does not fully explain what fans do.[4] K-pop fans' affective labor, as this book will trace, ranges in terms of intensity, investment, and impact. For some fans, K-pop is a hobby; for others, it can seem more like a full-time job. The industry actively pursues, and seeks to heighten, affective engagements. Indeed, it turns some kinds of engagements themselves into experiential products for sale; other kinds of affective engagements are shaped and promoted by industry practices that aim to materialize affective fan labor.

When I say that fans perform the *materialization* of affective labor, I mean to draw attention to various dimensions along which fan labor produces K-pop's mechanisms of connecting with consumers and expanding its cultural and economic footprint. *Material* is a term with multiple meanings and valences. In economics, material can refer to tangible goods and their value, whereas materialize in general parlance can also refer to producing something or making something appear or happen. To think about *performing* the materialization of affective labor, then, is to think about performance in and through which affective labor appears or happens, and also how affective labor itself produces consumer products and material value.

The book argues, first, that fans' affective labor plays a central role in creating the mediating platforms, dynamic content, and material culture and social sites of K-pop. This labor can be hard to recognize as such, because much of it takes place in and through the digital realm and via peer-to-peer interactions in cacophonous social media spaces. But this labor is essential to how K-pop's parasocial relationships transmute into meaningful personal and communal ones. In studies of popular culture, the term *parasocial* is used in different ways. Many conceptualize it as one-way relationships between fans and performers. However, I understood parasocial relationships as asymmetrical relationships—never entirely one-way, but two-way, asymmetric-yet-mutual attachments. Fan affective labor even shapes the kinds of affective labor expected of and performed by K-pop idols.

Second, fans' affective labor impacts K-pop's material structures in an economic sense. My study considers the ways different kinds of fan practices tend to materialize certain kinds of economic structures and relationships, namely globalized neoliberal capitalist ones. Gooyong Kim argues that K-pop fans and their affective labor not only promote and profit the industry, but are also exploited by it, and in doing so, show that fans lack genuine control over their activities.[5] But as we will see, this story is complex, as deokhu performances of affective labor can also cultivate individual fan subjectivities and collective actions that alter or push against neoliberal capitalist structures. Notably, attending to processes of materializing keeps affective labor's embodied and therefore gendered and racialized qualities in mind, even when these qualities might become harder to see in digital spaces.

Through considering the ways that performing deokhu links to the materialization of affective labor, this book contributes to scholarship by focusing on formations of fan subjectivity and community that foreground the agency of fans themselves—in contrast to popular (ageist, sexist, even often racist) portrayals of fans as brainwashed young girls whose actions are determined by technology, peer pressure, and slavish devotion to the K-pop industry. My centering labor in the study of performances of fandom, which has not yet been done anywhere near proportional to what fan labor produces, also offers new insights into the ways that performing deokhu intersects with neoliberal capitalist structures but can also depart from the industry's norms and goals. This study helps us better theorize the kinds of cultural, economic, social, and even political structures and relationships that K-pop fandom produces, as well as the work it does in generating individual subjectivities and collective communities that are forged in relationship to this industry but also exceed its parameters.

While there have been many shorter studies of K-pop fan culture, this is the first English-language academic monograph to analyze the creative efflorescence of K-pop fan practices through centering the framework of performing deokhu as affective labor. To evidence its claims, this study documents and provides close readings of various types of fan activities that I analyze through the lens of materializing affective labor. These include streaming music, voting, chatting with idols on fandom-associated smartphone apps, and creating new modes of fan videos. They also include organizing fan events such as exhibitions and meet-ups, independently publishing memoirs, participating in campaigns to influence or pressure the industry, and even filing complaints and lawsuits against idols. Through such activities, this book argues, fans have produced a kind of deokhu code—that is, a set of rules for fans to follow to support their favorite idols and connect with other fans, which therefore might also be thought of as a deokhu labor code that seeks to produce good relationships between asymmetrically positioned actors in the K-pop ecosystem. By illuminating a genre-spanning corpus of fan activities that has unfolded (and continues to unfold) over the past three decades, and by analyzing its contexts and contents, this study represents an important contribution to the making of a fan archive that is also an archive of affective labor.

To conduct this study, I combine insights from ethnography, cultural studies, fan studies, media studies, and performance studies. Significantly, I also draw on my own research as a participant-observer and co-performer witness. According to Dwight Conquergood and D. Soyini Madison, co-performer witnessing is a way of accessing cultural knowledge stored in the body.[6] It is therefore often useful for studying highly affectively charged cultural phenomena, such as K-pop fandom. By beginning below with an autobiographical account of becoming a K-pop deokhu in the late-1990s, and continuing to thread insights drawn from my experiences where relevant in subsequent chapters, I connect myself and my experience to generations of K-pop fans, showing at the same time how fandom practices have shifted over time. My participation in K-pop fan activities, which began in an era preceding widespread internet usage, smartphones, and social media (a first-person experience not often documented in English-language accounts of K-pop fandom), and which continues into the 2020s, gives me a long-term perspective on K-pop fan activities that helps me identify and understand vital moments in their evolution. Furthermore, my history as a fan and the knowledge I have acquired as such made it possible for me to enter certain spaces, understand the significance of certain protocols, notice changing norms, and discuss personal subjectivity as well as topics related to broader collective experiences. This paved the way for participant-observation and co-performer witnessing methodologies, which crucially allow for collaborating with fans whose communal pursuits have been stigmatized by dominant discourses that denigrate their activities as solely addictive, uncritical, and wasteful. Additionally, I have sought to solicit the stories and voices of otherwise marginalized and underrepresented fans and issues, drawing out and emphasizing differences of perspective in the cultural, intellectual, and social production of K-pop and fandom. For this research, 224 fans, aged between twenty and forty-five, and all identifying as female, were interviewed either in person in Korea or virtually from 2017 to 2024 to discuss their experiences as K-pop fans. While K-pop fandom spans genders and nationalities, my focus was on Korean women, as they constitute a central fan demographic whose labor plays important roles in the global expansion of K-pop fan practices. Participants were recruited through my existing social network and at concerts and fan events in various sites in Korea. The interviews were conducted in Korean, and all translations from Korean to English are my own. All interviewees have agreed to have their interviews printed anonymously in this book. Together, these research methodologies allow me to provide a multidimensional portrait of major continuities and transformations in K-pop fandom's evolving work of performing deokhu.

Confessions of a Deokhu Academic

April 15, 1997, is a date that I will never forget. It is the day that the Korean boy band SECHSKIES made their debut. Even if I forget my own name, I will still be using *19970415* as my bank account PIN or email password. K-pop fans joke that even after they have fallen out of love with their bias (their favorite star), the star's birthday or debut date will remain in their memory for life, like cherished souvenirs from the past.

In 1997, I was fourteen years old, in my second year of middle school in South Korea. I was the typical straight-A geek. And I was crazy about popular music. I could recite the top fifty K-pop songs in my sleep. My favorite TV shows were KBS's *Gayo Top 10*, MBC's *Inkigayo Best 50*, and SBS's *Inkigayo*—all weekly music programs that showcased new and popular K-pop acts and ranking charts based on popularity. I loved watching the stars sing and dance. I wanted to listen to their songs over and over again, but my allowance did not allow me to buy all the records I desired. My workaround was to wait for my favorite songs to play on the radio. The moment I heard the opening, I would rush over to my tape deck and start recording.

I listened to all genres—ballads, dance, house, and rap. Some of my favorite musicians, besides SECHSKIES, were 015B, Deux, Seo Taiji and Boys, Shin Seung-hun, and H.O.T. (High-Five of Teenagers). H.O.T. had made their debut a year earlier, in 1996, and were already South Korea's biggest boy band and its first idol group. Many of my classmates were members of CLUB H.O.T., its fan club. They kept up with all of H.O.T.'s appearances on TV and radio programs and could not wait to talk about them every day at school. They bought music magazines and traded articles about their favorite members. They even dressed like the band, carrying brightly colored accessories and wearing oversized baggy pants. Some girls went as far as visiting SM Entertainment—H.O.T.'s management agency—or the members' dorms and waited for them outside the buildings. I liked H.O.T.'s music, but I was not really interested in its members. When I saw one of my classmates dressed up in H.O.T.'s oversized bright red and yellow felt-tip hat, overalls, and mittens from their promotion for the song "Candy," I was perplexed by this level of devotion.

That changed on April 15, 1997.

SECHSKIES ("zeks-kees") is a portmanteau of the German words *sechs* and *kies*, which their management agency DSP translated as "six crystals." The band consists of six members—Eun Jiwon, Lee Jaijin, Kim Jae-duck, Kang Sung Hoon, Ko Ji Yong, and Jang Suwon, each with his own signature persona (e.g., leader, shy, cute, artistic). Like most first-generation K-pop groups, they barely had time to train before their debut, but were quite good. In the late 1990s, idols' singing skills and lip-synching on TV were controversial issues, so SECHSKIES mostly performed live and always liked to ad-lib. The best Korean songwriters wrote for them, so all the tracks on their albums were good. Although their specialty was dance music, their albums covered a range of genres. From 1997 until the band broke up in May 2000, SECHSKIES released five full studio albums, performed in the children's musical *Ali Baba and the Forty Thieves* (April 25 to May 5, 1998), starred in the film *Seventeen* (released on July 17, 1998), and even performed in North Korea (December 5, 1999). Unlike most idols whose work was little known outside their fandom, the track "Couple" from their *Special Album* became a nationwide hit. In many ways, the band was a trailblazer in K-pop idol culture.

I loved SECHSKIES not only because the members and their music were awesome, but also because they gave me something to hold onto every day. That was probably my *ipdeok*—beginning *deokjil* ("fanning") or entering the fandom—and start of becoming a deokhu. Derived from the Japanese term *otaku*, which means "a person having an intense or obsessive interest especially in the fields of anime and manga," *deokhu* is a Korean slang for an avid, enthusiastic fan.[7] I went through a short period of *ipdeokbujeonggi*—a portmanteau of *ipdeok* and *bujeonggi* ("denial period"), meaning a period of denial some K-pop fans experience before embracing their identity as a deokhu. Those unsure about becoming a fan would *ganjaep*—dabble in or dip one's toes in fanning—before making up one's mind about becoming a deokhu. Idol fandom culture was often ridiculed by adults and the mainstream media, but it was a strong subculture among Korean teens, especially girls. Maybe that was even part of the appeal for many of us.

When I was in middle school, most of the Korean parents I knew seemed very conservative, as though all they cared about was getting their children into a prestigious university. My friends and I all had the same option: to get into a good university, or graduate high school and get a job. I do not think I had any friends whose parents said, "Of course, since you like make-up so much, you could go to cosmetology school." They all said, "Of course, since you like make-up so much, you could get into a good university and study design or something" or "Get into a good university, and then we will talk."

We were all required to go to classes from Monday to Friday, and half a day on Saturday, and study hard. We took courses in Korean, English, math, science, social studies, history, ethics, music, art, physical education, home economics, and Chinese letters. Except for physical education, all classes were lectures, with no discussion or group work. Fifty students were crammed into a small classroom, with two students at each wooden desk. Although Korean public education is great in terms of instilling knowledge in students, in my experience, it tends to stamp out creativity, individuality, and critical thinking. No wonder, then, that we related to songs like Seo Taiji and Boys' "Gyosil Idea" (Classroom idea), SECHSKIES's "Hagwon byeolgok" (School anthem), and H.O.T.'s "Yeolmatchwo" (Line up!), which criticize the unnecessary competitiveness of the Korean education system and the stress it places on students. We also had very few extracurricular activities. Except for a few students who were selected to join the Broadcasting Club and the members of the Student Council, there were no other school activities. We just went to classes, ate lunch, had more classes, cleaned the classroom, and went home. Some of my friends had after-school tutoring or instruction at private institutions. For me, listening to K-pop and fanning SECHSKIES became my main sources of fun.

The Korean media tried to analyze our generation often describing us as headstrong and unique (meaning rude and weird). Then the 1997 Asian financial crisis struck. Millions of workers were laid off, and hundreds of them took their own lives. The evening news broadcasted how fast the economy was plummeting. One of my classmates told me that her father had lost his business and her family had nothing to eat but noodles. We were too young to understand everything that was going on, and there was nothing that we could do except study: but, with the economy in freefall, what were we studying for? For many of us, fanning K-pop was an escape from reality. When we listened to the saccharine music and lost ourselves in the idols' stage performances, we could forget about everything else. It was just easier to choose to love something that energized us. While teachers scolded us for paying more attention to bands than our studies, and our parents blamed the idols when our grades dropped, K-pop was too alluring to ignore. K-pop set teens apart from the older generation mired in the financial crises, while also bringing us together.

Attending an all-girls' middle school was a blessing. It was practically a big K-pop boot camp. My friends and I had similar routines. Our school uniform was a hideous gray blazer and skirt and white shirt with ruffles, regulation hairdo, the same class schedules, and plans to get into a good university. What distinguished us from one another was our biases—that is, our favorite idols. The first rule of K-pop fanning was if your bias was part of a group, you had to love the entire group. My favorite group was SECHSKIES and my *choeae*—the Korean word for bias—was Jiwon. I also loved the other five members, but he was my choeae. In the early days, being an *akgae*—a portmanteau of *akseong* (toxic) and *gaeinpaen* (individual fan), meaning a fan who only cares about one member out of the group—was not tolerated in K-pop fandom.

Almost everyone had a bias. While many students loved popular idols like H.O.T., SECHSKIES, Yoo Seung-jun, and SHINHWA, some students preferred less popular acts like Cool, Turbo, and Jinusean. Students with the same bias would automatically become your friends because it was so fun to talk about what the bias had just said or done. Friends would also sing and dance together. During the lunch break, I would sing with other SECHSKIES fans or practice the group's intricate choreography. Sometimes, we would pool our allowances and go to karaoke. Minors were not allowed to enter karaoke without adult supervision, but there were parlors near my school that let us in. In those small rooms that stank of cigarettes and had fuzzy red couches with all kinds of stains, my friends and I would each belt out our bias's part. It did not matter whether we were good or not; it was just fun.

The second rule of K-pop fans was to love only one group at a time. This rule is no longer followed or enforced, but it was in the 1990s. We were expected to be very loyal to our one and only favorite group. If someone talked shit about them, we were expected to fight. This was quite unfortunate for me because deep down, I was a *japdeok*—a multi-fan who appreciates different groups. I really liked H.O.T.'s music, with its cool and smooth edge, and composer Yoo Young-jin's signature style. I bought all their cassette tapes and listened to them at home. I memorized their lyrics booklet. Of course, SECHSKIES's music was great, but so was H.O.T.'s music; yet, I did not dare to take anything related to H.O.T. to school because of the fierce competition between the two groups and their fandoms. The fight scenes in the Korean TV drama *Reply 1997*, in which H.O.T. and SECHSKIES fans pull each other's hair out, are not far from the truth. Admitting that I loved both H.O.T. and SECHSKIES's music would have cost me friends on both sides, so I kept this secret.

One of my most important fan activities was creating my own "merchandise." K-pop companies at this time did not release much official swag besides the full studio albums and fan club kit. Instead, stationery stores near schools sold unofficial merchandise, mostly photos. The store in front of my school sold SECHSKIES photos for 400–500 won each (less than 50 cents). Fans who wanted to show off their biases created their own merchandise with photos and pages they had torn out of magazines. Sometimes they would wrap their textbooks with transparent vinyl (to protect them) and insert a photo of their bias on the cover. Some fans would use thick paper to create their own pencil cases and adorn the surface with photos of their bias. Others created their own pins. Fans would also use a six-hole-punch journal to keep track of their bias's schedule and decorate it with photos and stickers. Making your own merchandise was fun, and everyone's creations were different. An equivalent fan activity that is popular today would be *polkku* or *tapkku*, which are decorating K-pop photo card holders and sleeves.

Back then, it was not just merchandise that was difficult to find—so was information on the idols' schedules or public appearances. When I was a new SECHSKIES fan, I would borrow the TV section of my parents' newspaper every morning and see if there were any announcements about SECHSKIES's appearance on a TV show. At school, I would ask my friends if they had heard anything. In the evenings, I tried listening to all radio stations for a few minutes to see if SECHSKIES would make an appearance. After a few months, I learned about the 152 *saseoham*—a pre-recorded phone message—where I could call 152–2580 and get the group's schedule. In the days before the internet, the 152 phone messages were the only way to receive information quickly. The few lucky friends who had personal computers could use *PC tongshin*, which is basically the early version of dial-up Internet access and text-based Internet system. My parents did not let me have a PC tongshin service. But my friend Hana, who was a Jinusean fan, had Hitel installed on her computer and would sometimes print out the messages that the SECHSKIES members had posted on the Hitel fan club. Whenever Hana brought me those posts, I was so grateful to have such an important fan resource in my hands. Nowadays, idols' schedules are easily accessible via official social media accounts that are run by management companies.

Using the 152 phone messages and intelligence gathered from my friends made it possible to figure out when and where SECHSKIES would be on TV and the radio. Once I had their schedule, I would then have to figure out when I would tell my father that I needed to change the TV channel. When it was time for the music program to start, I would muster up my courage and ask meekly, "Um, Dad? I really need to watch *Inkigayo* now." If my father did not care what was on TV, he would grunt and hand me the remote control. If he was watching something that he wanted to watch, he would ask, "Why in the world would you watch something useless like that? Look at those kids screaming there, throwing their life away instead of studying." If my family had had more than one television set, this would have been avoided. My friends and I started to record the music programs with VHS tapes and then swap them when we could not watch the show because of some remote-hogging family member. When I could watch the music shows in peace, I made sure to vote for SECHSKIES if they were vying for first place that week. Fans always voted by phone during the show. Perched on the sofa, I would wait to see if SECHSKIES's song was a candidate for No. 1, and if it was, I would grab the phone and dial the number. That was one of the few ways I could support my idol. Today, voting has become one of the most common fan activities, with fandoms organizing collective labor to vote not only on TV programs and annual music awards, but also through fandom-associated smartphone apps.

Monthly music magazines were another important source of information for K-pop fans. Music magazines such as *Music Life*, *Pastel*, *Photo Music*, *Tomato*, and *Zzang* carried the latest news about idols as well as information on merchandise-making, pen pals, and other resources for participating in K-pop culture. Their prices ranged from 4,500 to 6,000 won ($4 to $5), which was not cheap for students. My friends and I helped each other out. For example, if I bought the latest issue of *Music Life*, I would tear out the pages of H.O.T. interviews and give them to my friends who were CLUB H.O.T. If one of those friends bought a different magazine, she would tear out the SECHSKIES interviews for me. Similar practices continue today, now in response to the endless supply of merchandise that K-pop companies produce, with fans of different biases teaming up to buy and *buncheol*—divide up and distribute—merchandise or photo cards.

The magazines I read reported on the most trivial details about idols, such as their height and weight, favorite food, and ideal type of potential dating partner. I read SECHSKIES's interviews so many times that I knew the answers by heart. In hindsight, I suspect that the band's managers or PR team scripted the interviews—for instance, even though some K-pop boy idols may not have wanted to date girls, or already had partners, management companies had a stake in controlling the public image of their sexuality in a way that was most marketable, or at least unlikely to cause controversy.

These magazines also helped fans form communities during the pre-digital, pre-internet era. In the back of the magazine, there was a section where fans could advertise for pen pals. Each time I purchased a magazine, I would read the pen pal section carefully, looking for another SECHSKIES fan. After reading numerous pen pal ads, I wrote letters to two other SECHSKIES fans with whom I corresponded for a few years until my parents installed dial-up internet access. Then, I was able to sign up for an email address and visit fan websites via search engines such as Yahoo! Korea and Lycos Korea. Until then, my two pen pals and I exchanged stories of fanning and sent each other small gifts such as SECHSKIES magazine clippings and photos. Because these pen pals lived in other Korean cities, I did not have a chance to meet with them in person. However, I felt a strong connection with them as we confessed our love for SECHSKIES in letter after letter. Although it took time and patience, I was always overjoyed to receive their letters.

Our teachers and parents disapproved of K-pop magazines, so my friends and I were careful to keep them hidden. We would usually look at them over our lunch break and keep our personal collections stowed away. I also bought several A4 files and carefully slipped the ripped-out magazine pages into the transparent sleeves. They were my prized possessions. Later, at some point when my family was moving or when I was studying abroad, the files were lost. Now, I have only the CDs, concert videos, and a handful of merchandise from that time.

Concert and musical tickets were sold at Je-il Bank branches for 25,000 won (about $20). To reserve good seats, we had to get to the bank early and stand in line before it opened at 9 a.m. Many fans brought sleeping bags, waiting in line for days. I was very envious of them. If I were to do that, my parents would have created a scene, dragged me home, and then grounded me for the rest of my life. I settled for sneaking out of the house at the crack of dawn the day the tickets went on sale. One time, when I arrived at the bank, there was a line that went around the block; it was not even seven o'clock yet. When it was time for the bank to open, the fans who had been camped out all night on the sidewalk stood up and stretched. Everyone was giddy with excitement. When the doors opened, the chatter increased. A nervous-looking employee ordered the fans to get in line. After what it seemed like an eternity, it was finally my turn. A tired employee mumbled, "I will help you reserve your ticket," without looking up. Trembling with excitement, I handed her the 25,000 won I had carefully saved over the past few weeks. After a few clicks, I had my ticket. I accepted it with both hands, out of deference. Outside the bank, I stared at it. I was going to the SECHSKIES concert! I could not tell where my seat was, but I did not care. The ticket would get me into the stadium. I tucked it safely into my bag and skipped home.

Some fans say that they are glad not to have to wait in line in days for tickets anymore, since they can get them online. Maybe, maybe not. *Tiketting*—reserving or purchasing tickets—is often referred to as *piketting*—tiketting so competitive that it is like a bloodthirsty war. When I am able to

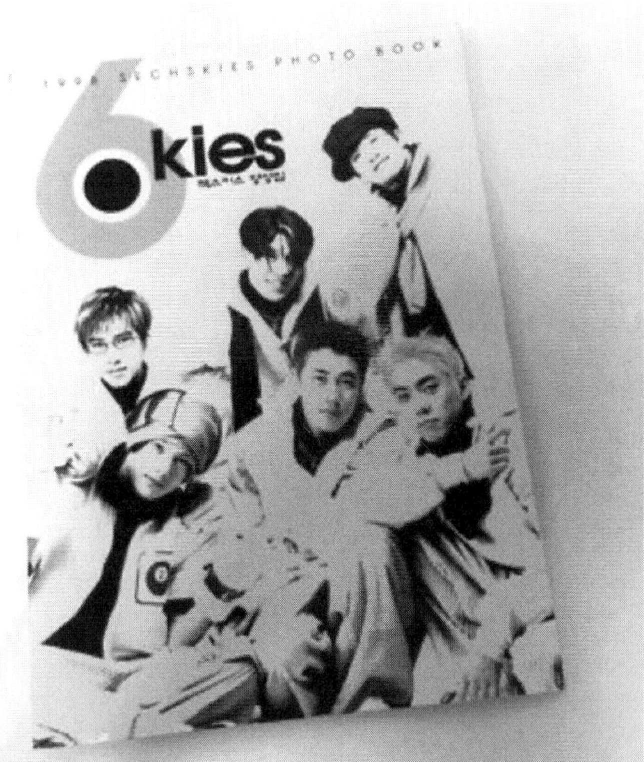

Figure 1. SECHSKIES's 1998 photo book. Photo by Areum Jeong.

score really good seats from Auction Ticket, Interpark Ticket, Melon Ticket, or Yes24 Ticket, I thank my lucky stars that I did not have to stand in line for them. But when there are people—*daeri tiketting* or *daelti*—who use macro programs to reserve seats just to resell them at a huge markup, I curse and think I would rather have the line. I hope there is a special place in hell for people who do that. However, I see more and more fans today using their services not only for tiketting, but also to attend TV program tapings. Attending TV program tapings is similar to tiketting in that fans must promptly sign up by commenting on posts or online forms created by management agencies. The competition for signing up on these forms or posts has become so fierce that fans refer to them as *daennim*—comment Olympics—or *pomnim*—form Olympics. But before all this, I went to concerts, musicals, and autograph signings, watching SECHSKIES from a distance. Getting nearer to the group would have required days of standing in line,

Figure 2. SECHSKIES's 1999 concert VCD. Photo by Areum Jeong.

which was always impossible for me. Still, I wanted more than anything to see them up close.

And then, in 1998, I did.

SECHSKIES's movie *Seventeen* was about to be released. I tried finding a way to get into a premiere, but couldn't. My mother must have noticed my disappointment and asked me what was wrong. I admitted that I really wanted to go to the premiere, but did not know how I could. "Is that all?" she asked. "Tell me the number of their management agency." Startled, I wrote down the number, which I knew by heart. Mom called. "Hello, thank you for your work," she said in her most charming voice. "My daughter is a huge SECHSKIES fan and the top student in her class. She really wants to attend the movie premiere and I was wondering if there was a way for us to go." I stared at her in disbelief. Did she really think that DSP was going to hand out premiere passes because I was a straight-A student? She listened for a minute. "Uh-huh, uh-huh. Great, thank you so much and have a good day!" Then she jotted something down and hung up the phone. I was too dumbstruck to say a word. "Well," my mother said, "the very nice lady said that if you are the top student in your class, you definitely deserve to go! She said she would put our names on the list." I jumped up and down, hugging my mom. To this day, I consider it the greatest thing she has ever done for me.

On July 17, 1998, Mom and I went to the movie theater near Namsan in Seoul. We went right from school, so I was still in my uniform. When we arrived, there was already a line of excited girls near the entrance. They were probably the most enthusiastic fan club members. Feeling geeky and shy, and also out of place since I was there with my mom, I hung back. When a staff member showed up, Mom went up to her and introduced herself, reminding her of their phone conversation. The staff looked at me and smiled and said, "Sure, why don't Mom and you wait over there? When the fan club goes in, you can follow them." I nodded and whispered a thank you. Mom and I waited near a staircase.

Then, without any notice, the SECHSKIES members ascended the stairs. I was close enough to touch them. Ji Yong was the first to appear; I had never seen anyone so handsome. I gasped; my mother later told me that my face went completely pale. It was the only time in my life that I felt time stand still. Next followed Jiwon, Sung Hoon, and the other members. They strolled past me and into the theater. I stared at them until they were out of my sight. When I came back to my senses, I heard the shrieks of the fan club members who were still standing in line. I was so amazed and grateful that I saw the members of my favorite band up close. I hugged my Mom and promised that I would listen to everything she said. Although I have had some lapses, I meant it at the time. What I experienced could never happen today because giving special treatment to a fan is not tolerated in the fandom. But it was the best day of my life.

After the premiere, I decided to hang out with Myeong-ju, another student in our school, to find out more about SECHSKIES. She was a *sasaeng* (an obsessive, stalker-like fan) who often went to the members' homes and waited for them outside. There were always girls camped out in front of idols' dorms or apartments back then. Although there are now laws against stalking, back then what we were doing was considered harmless. Because we were in different classes, I introduced myself to Myeong-ju as a SECHSKIES fan. She was delighted. She told me that she often went to the members' apartments and invited me to go with her the next time. I could hardly conceal my joy at the invitation.

One day, when we did not have afternoon classes, Myeong-ju and I took the subway to Ichon station. We got out at Exit 4 and walked down the tree-lined streets. Myeong-ju gave me a tour of the neighborhood where Sung Hoon and Ji Yong had grown up and where they were still living at that time. "That's where Sung Hoon and Ji Yong went to elementary school!" "That's where Ji Yong went to middle school!" It felt surreal to actually see the places that I had only heard of or read about in magazines. I also realized how sheltered my life had been. I was born in Korea and raised in New Jersey, but after I returned to Korea and enrolling in elementary school and middle school, my daily life hardly went beyond the boundaries of Galhyeon-dong, a small neighborhood in the northwestern part of Seoul that was not well-known for anything. Ichon-dong was not far from my neighborhood, and it suddenly dawned on me that I never thought of the other neighborhoods in Seoul much less considered visiting them. My life consisted of going to school, coming home, doing homework, and watching TV or listening to music. I did not like changes even in my daily routine and still don't like venturing out of my comfort zone. But this outing was worth it.

"That's where Sung Hoon lives!" Myeong-ju pointed to an apartment complex. "Oh, wow!" I could not take my eyes off the building. "Yeah, but he's probably not home right now," Myeong-ju said as she marched ahead. Every step she took was confident. She was as familiar with the neighborhood as any of its lifelong residents. We turned around a corner and approached an apartment complex with the words Mi-ju Mansion painted on the side. "This is where Ji Yong lives," Myeong-ju announced, stopping in front of the entrance. No other fans were there; they were probably still in school. She looked around cautiously. "The apartment guard doesn't like fans so we should be quiet. If he sees us, he might yell at us."

"So . . . do we just wait here?" I asked.

"Yeah. I once waited all night to see him. They often come home very late after schedules." I imagined what my parents would do to me if I camped out in front of an idol's home all night. Myeong-ju and I stood in front of the apartment and spoke quietly to each other for about twenty minutes. Then, Myeong-ju looked up and gasped. "It's Ji Yong's older sister, Hye-na!" I glanced up and saw a young woman who looked like a college student walking out of the apartment, heading in our direction. When she came closer, Myeong-ju jumped up and down. "Hello, Hye-na unni!" The woman's pace slowed down and she eyed us warily. "Hello, Hye-na unni! I'm Ji Yong's fan! We met a few weeks ago!" Myeong-ju chirped as if she was an old family friend.

A look of recognition washed over the young woman's face. "Ah, yes, hello." She smiled. Not knowing what to do when meeting your idol's family member for the first time, I bowed politely. "Hello, I'm also a fan of Ji Yong. This is my first time here." She looked at me and smiled.

"I'm afraid Ji Yong is not home right now. He was already gone when I got up."

"It's ok. Where are you going, unni?"

"I'm going to classes."

"Unni, may we accompany you to the subway station?" Myeong-ju asked.

"Um, sure." So Myeong-ju and I walked with Hye-na to Ichon station. I didn't think that I should ask her about Ji Yong, so I started asking questions about her. "Unni, are you a college student?"

"Yes, I study design at X University."

"Oh, cool!" We chatted about university life until we arrived at the subway station.

"Unni, would you mind signing my journal?" I asked shyly. I handed her my SECHSKIES fan club journal and a pen. She smiled and wrote "Please love and support Ji Yong. From Hye-na Ko." I did not have an autograph from any SECHSKIES members back then, so what Hye-na wrote for me was very special.

Hye-na must have been tired of all the fans camping outside her home, yet she was very kind to two middle school girls she did not know. After we waved bye to Hye-na, Myeong-ju decided to go back to Ji Yong's apartment and wait for him, while I decided to go home. Waiting in front of his home for twenty minutes had been long enough for me. I had some newfound respect for fans who could endure hours of boredom. As we parted ways, Myeong-ju asked to borrow 3,000 won ($2). She promised to pay me back the next Monday. I knew that she wouldn't but handed her the money anyway, because the time with her had been worthwhile. Later on, I visited Ji Yong, Sung Hoon, and Jiwon's homes a few times by myself. Each time, I remembered to bring a book and my cassette player.

After I graduated from middle school, my family moved to Hanshin Apartment in Banpo-dong. I had been accepted to Daewon Foreign Language High School, one of the most prestigious high schools in Korea, with a merit scholarship. My parents were thrilled, so they were happy to move to a new neighborhood to be closer to the high school. What none of us knew was that Suwon lived in the same apartment complex as well. It was a dream come true! I had already found out where all the members lived through the other fans. Jiwon lived in Shin-gil-dong, near Seong-ae Hospital. Sung Hoon lived in Hyundai Apartment Building 21, Unit 501, in Ichon-dong. Jaijin and Jae-duck lived in the dorm in Bangbae-dong, near Bangbae Middle School. It took me almost a year to collect all this information.

In the new apartment complex, I lived in Building 14 and Suwon lived in Building 29. The day we moved in, when my parents were busy with the movers, I asked if I could explore. "Yes, but don't go too far away," my mom replied absentmindedly. I headed toward Building 29 and stepped into the entrance, looking at the apartment guard. Then I squared my shoulders. I was a resident of this apartment complex! If someone asked, I could tell them that and say I was visiting a friend. I stepped into the elevator and pressed the button to the twelfth floor. A bunch of girls were sitting in front of Unit 1209. We greeted each other. Some of them had been there for hours, and others had just arrived. One girl had come all the way from Busan. When I told the group that I lived in the complex, they were impressed and told me how lucky I was. To me, it was a bigger deal than being accepted into that prestigious high school.

Although Suwon was not my bias, there were definitely perks that came with living in the same complex as him. I had met Sung Hoon, Ji Yong's older sister, and Suwon's older brother, but I had still not seen the love of my life, Jiwon, up close (except briefly at the movie premiere). Whenever I went to his house, he was not there. Then, one day, as I was returning from school, I glanced at Building 29 and spotted the SECHSKIES van in the parking lot. I rushed over. Another girl was already peering inside the van. The windows were tinted, but I could still see someone sleeping in the front passenger seat. My heart started pounding. It was Jiwon. I did not dare tap the windows or wake him because I did not want to disturb him. I stood there and just stared at his gorgeous face, mere inches away from me, only a glass window between us. I could see his smooth dark skin, handsome features, and long eyelashes that created a shadow under his closed eyelids. I must have stood there for fifteen minutes when SECHSKIES's manager approached the van with Suwon. He must have picked Jiwon up first. The other girl and I jumped away from the van. The manager and Suwon got into the van and drove off. The two of us watched the van disappear into the distance.

My fan life didn't end when SECHSKIES disbanded in 2000 or when I graduated high school. I continued to support Jiwon's solo activities and career transitions for more than twenty years. And in 2016, the group miraculously reunited. I fanned harder than ever, trying to savor every moment.

And because I have a big heart full of love for K-pop, I also fanned other groups and musicians as I grew older. My love for K-pop eventually led me to become an academic who researches and teaches classes on Korean popular culture. This book brings together my career as researcher and my decades-long work of performing deokhu.

The Evolution of Deokhu Labor

Short for "Korean popular music," K-pop does not have a fixed definition, and scholars have tried to define K-pop in their own ways. For example, Suk-Young Kim calls K-pop a "multimedia performance," meaning that not only is K-pop about infectious music and pleasing vocal ability, but it is also about dance, fashion, and spectacular visuality.[8] Youna Kim calls K-pop "total entertainment," meaning that K-pop encompasses all entertainment forms: music, dance, television, movies, advertisements and more, with much of this performance happening digitally and online.[9] While these definitions consider the industrial ecology and digitized platforms, they do not include the fans who promote said industry by performing labor on such platforms. As for me, I define K-pop along three dimensions. First, it is a cultural product generated by music industry agencies, which are embedded within a neoliberal capitalist entertainment industry with national and transnational dimensions. Second, K-pop is a receptive phenomenon, by which I mean that the reach and import of K-pop comes from its resonance with individual and collective audiences who propel its phenomenal success. And thirdly, it is a community that is held together and shaped primarily by fandom and its labor.

While fandom has been viewed as central to numerous subcultures based around entertainment commodities, the ways in which fans organize and perform fan labor are considered central and distinctive to the phenomenon called K-pop. Because this book focuses on fan activities and practices performed by idol group fandoms in particular, it is necessary to explain K-pop

Figure 3. Eun Jiwon solo's albums. Photo by Areum Jeong.

Figure 4. My collection of SECHSKIES and Eun Jiwon albums and merchandise. Photo by Areum Jeong.

idol fan culture, which is both similar to and different from related industries such as J-pop. K-pop's idol production system was influenced by that of Japan. The term *idol* was first popularized in Japan in 1963, and idols came to be mass-produced in 1971.[10] In his extensive research, Patrick Galbraith explains that J-pop idols make themselves accessible to fans through live performances, small venues, and special events where contact and communication are possible.[11] The relationship between idols and fans is characterized by intimacy; fans get to know more, and come to care more, about idols. Galbraith also argues that Japanese idols in global circulation have many limitations "not only because of language barriers, but also because of divergent production and promotion strategies."[12] While the idol industries of K-pop and J-pop hold many similarities, K-pop localized and further developed the idol production system, which in turn influences that of Japan today and also exerts unprecedented global reach. K-pop idols make themselves accessible to fans through communication via digital media and technology, where much of fan labor takes place. While K-pop incorporates acts beyond idol groups, K-pop fandom is often organized around supporting idols and idol groups, and this is the aspect of K-pop that I focus on.

Further comparisons to J-pop help historicize the emergence of K-pop while also marking what is distinctive about it. Hiroshi Aoyagi focuses on how Japan's idol-manufacturing industry absorbs young people into its system of production, molds their selves into marketable personalities, commercializes their images for the masses, and contributes to the ongoing construction of ideal images of adolescent selfhood.[13] This capitalization process is commercial, social, and cultural at the same time.[14] Aoyagi looks at how Japanese fans "contribute" to the idol industry by "following," "awaiting," and "supporting" their favorite idols through acts of commodity fetishism/consumption.[15] Aoyagi's perspective on Japanese fans' being limited to secondary or supporting roles in the idol industry is starkly different from how many scholars, including myself, see K-pop fans as content creators who help promote the industry as much as an audience who consumes the industry's products.

For more than two decades, scholars have studied how K-pop fan culture and fan practices evolved and transformed in Korea and beyond. Min-Woo Jung and Na-Young Lee examined how K-pop fan practices, which were previously mainly viewed as merely passive acts, evolved into a kind of "prosumer" activity—a term that combines *producer* and *consumer*—that influences and manages idols.[16] As Sooah Kim explains, this evolution transformed into a widespread phenomenon with the emergence of audition TV programs, where fans' support became—and remains—crucially important.[17] Thus, JungBong Choi and Roald Maliangkay define fans as "a massive, loosely connected collective, whose cultural endeavors traverse the curatorial, re/distributive, artistic, and consumptive spheres," and as "trailblazers, expanding the cultural breadth and depth of K-pop products."[18] In summary, today K-pop fans are widely understood, both by scholars but also by producers of K-pop, as proactive and productive agents in the industry. From here, we can better consider why and how fandom practices should be construed as materializing affective labor.

K-pop fans from Korea and beyond show similarities in their affective practices of supporting idols and expressing happiness and pleasure with other fans through digital activities. Michelle Cho analyzes how BTS and their fans expand and share forms of mediated liveness—through "real-live contents," archiving liveness in reaction videos, screen-sharing and fancams—and how such practices reveal "a desire for collectivity."[19] In a similar manner, Rebecca Chiyoko King-O'Riain explores how the idea of liveness continues to be important in facilitating emotional closeness with idols and interactions with other fans.[20] Courtney McLaren and Dal Yong Jin also emphasize how the use of social media is instrumental to fan practices in consuming idol content, arguing that "hybridized popular culture is circulated not only through transnational flows of content but also transcultural constructions of affective investment and identity."[21] The digital setting enables fans to promote their activities via online spaces. While fans support their favorite idols, K-pop also becomes a space for fans to express their gender identities and sexualities[22] and perform activism.[23]

Notably, K-pop fandom cannot be fully theorized through the work of Euro-American-focused fan studies scholars, such as Henry Jenkins and others, due to the complexities and cultural specificities of K-pop fan culture. Sujeong Kim and Sooah Kim explain that culturally specific phenomena in K-pop fandom, such as the high premium placed on authenticity and intimacy in idol-fan relationships, fandom's networked and organized activities to support their favorite idols, and fandom's voluntary regulations of *sasaeng* (stalker fans), requires analysis that goes beyond simply utilizing Western-centric frameworks.[24] I fully concur with these two scholars, and this is precisely why we need to take a closer look at K-pop fan culture to expand the ways we theorize global fan culture and media, including its relations of labor. And this is also why this book focuses on female Korean fans, which will hopefully open paths to further studies of K-pop fan labor across a broader global scale.

Expanding ideas of parasociality in fan-idol relationships is key in understanding K-pop fan culture. David Horton and Richard Wohl first described parasocial interaction as the psychological connection that audiences form with media figures, especially in television.[25] Repeated exposure to a media persona can transform this parasocial interaction into a parasocial relationship, characterized by feelings of friendship, identification, and intimacy on the part of audience members.[26] The media figure's self-disclosure—for example, the media figure's appearances as "themselves" across other venues, such as talk shows and social media accounts—can enhance these connections, creating a strong sense of attachment and loyalty among audiences that resembles their relationships with close friends. Yet the traditional concept of parasocial relationship was viewed as one-sided, excluding any ideas of reciprocal interaction between the media persona and viewer. As such, it has sometimes also been pathologized. Rivkah Groszman draws attention to the state of parasocial theory being viewed negatively when applied to fan behavior, especially in K-pop.[27] Arguing against such notions, Groszman writes that parasocial relationships can help form connections not only with media figures but also help foster communities with other fans. Recent scholarship aims to reconceptualize traditional understandings of parasociality in light of the growth and popularity of live-streaming and social media platforms today. Scholars argue that such platforms are "no longer traditionally one-sided" and can create reciprocal communication between the media persona and viewer through parasocial relationships that combine roles of "wishful identification, emotional engagement, community affiliation, fandom cultures, and increased presence and accessibility."[28] Following such conversations, this book aims to examine the unique relationships between fan and idol, and the types of fan labor that are involved in shaping these relationships within the neoliberal capitalist K-pop industry, which promotes and relies upon such materialization of affective labor.

While records of fans of celebrities in Korea go back as far as the colonial period, with fans of *byeonsa* (silent-film narrator) performers, specific political-economic and sociopolitical conditions have shaped the deokhu culture since the early 1990s that are important to elaborate.[29] It is widely understood that most aspects of K-pop are enmeshed in the neoliberal capitalist structures and aims of the industry. Historically speaking, the K-pop industry emerged and developed in tandem with South Korea's neoliberal capitalist economy. Neoliberal ideology and policies advocate for a society where political and economic structures are primarily liberal and capitalist, yet are balanced by a democracy with constitutional limits and a minimal welfare state. Neoliberals emphasize the importance of individual freedoms and a market-driven economy as key drivers of both personal liberty and economic success. Scholars such as Gooyong Kim argue that K-pop has been "conditioned to prosper while the state is in charge of reconstructing its national economy to accommodate neoliberal challenges for economic development."[30] While Kim mainly focuses on K-pop female idols, his discussion of K-pop's being "an integral part of neoliberalism's grand transformative project that turns society into a massive marketplace by conditioning the audience's value system and code of thoughts and conducts" is something to consider when examining how K-pop fans form affective attachments to male idols as well and participate in unpaid fan labor that aligns with the neoliberal capitalist industry's aims.[31]

In terms of sociopolitical factors, the concept of a "new generation" that emerged in the decade of the 1990s in Korea also provided an important background for K-pop's deokhu subculture and the kinds of work it has performed.[32]

Emerging from the ashes and specters of the dictatorship period of the 1970s and 1980s, Korean corporations and mass media of the early 1990s constructed the image of *sinsedae* (new generation) to meet various needs.[33] Those belonging to the sinsedae generation were viewed as young people who enjoyed and valued a sense of freedom. And perhaps more importantly, they were characterized as having stronger and broader consumption needs than the elder generation.[34] However, this kind of new communal identity was not always viewed in a positive light. For instance, when chaos ensued at a concert by the American boy band New Kids on the Block in Korea in 1992, the elder generation and the mass media bemoaned sinsedae behavior and values, with K-pop emerging as both a site for youth sociality and a target of intergenerational complaints.[35]

Amid this kind of atmosphere, Seo Taiji and Boys, a popular act that made their debut in 1992, defiantly pushed back against such negative views of the younger generation. The group represented the colorful fluorescence of sinsedae—a combination of capitalist consumerism supported by the corporations and mass media, the desire for a sense of freedom and newness, and defiance of the elder generation's authority—and the group's fandom laid the ground for K-pop fan culture in Korea. In this sense, it is no surprise that hits by first generation idol groups include songs about pushing against educational and social systems from the younger generation's viewpoints, as seen in H.O.T.'s "Warrior's Descendant," "We Are the Future," "Wolf and Sheep," "Line Up!," and SECHSKIES's "School Anthem."

At the same time, K-pop tapped into and reflected young women's desires and needs in the masculine and patriarchal Korean society. Although K-pop as a subculture was often dismissed and looked down upon and fans were viewed in an ageist and misogynist light, its growing importance was impossible to ignore. As this subculture transformed into one of the biggest pop culture phenomena in the world, it became increasingly obvious that none of this growth would have been possible without the blood, sweat, and tears of young women whose fan labor shaped K-pop from its birth. In the beginning, many deokhu were Korean schoolgirls, like myself; but as K-pop's fandom grew, performing deokhu became a more diverse and more global phenomenon. While the majority of K-pop fans are young women, and the deokhu subculture is, in many ways, still viewed largely as a normatively heterosexual "girls' subculture," its demography is expanding to include diverse genders, nationalities, and sexualities.

Considering the demographic diversity and global spread of its variously positioned and invested members, it is important not to essentialize K-pop fandom. Yet, some important similarities and connections characterize the deokhu, which can perhaps best be variously thought of as both an identity enacted by individuals and a representational shorthand for a certain set of fandom norms and practices, which are always shifting in response to sociocultural and economic conditions. My research considers the deokhu as:

- a receptive fan who consumes K-pop via various media platforms and is, therefore, inclined to develop parasocial relationships, especially (but not only) through digital means

- an active agent who has the ability to influence others via collective action performed in and among, but also beyond, the fandom
- an active consumer—or, more specifically, a *prosumer* who participates in producing what is being consumed—who engages with the neoliberal, capitalist industry that is K-pop (and might hold or appear to hold consumer capitalist attitudes)
- a participant in mass culture who is likely to be dismissed, looked down upon, mocked, or scorned due to the ageist, sexist, misogynist, and sometimes racist beliefs that are common among non-fans and prevalent in industry and media discourse

The deokhu is constructed by external ideas and images of fandom, and through repeated acts of experiencing, learning, performing, and sharing K-pop fandom's dynamic communal aims, characteristics, cultures, missions, and values. Through participation in K-pop fan communities and the codes that shape them, a fan develops an identity and subjectivity that crystallizes in and is expressed through individual and collective performances of deokhu. These performances, which take a variety of forms, including labor-based ones, materialize the affective entanglements between idols and fans that are ultimately at the heart of deokhu subjectivity and the K-pop industry.

In prioritizing a Korean-language term for what is now an international and multilingual phenomenon of K-pop fandom, I aim to center the particular significance that Korean fans have played in shaping broader deokhu practices. As we will see, Korean fans have pioneered and performed particular types of fan labor that draw on their specific cultural positioning and knowledge; for instance, they play crucial roles in helping fans in other places understand the Korean entertainment industry and its metrics of success, and in providing information that international fans use to guide their own engagements with K-pop and shape its industrial trajectories. In doing so, they materialize what might be called transnational or translational affective labor, which can be thought of as labor that creates greater possibilities for the international community to form through and within transnational fandom culture.[36] Of course, there are other groups of fans who provide other kinds of crucial labor aimed at making K-pop a more inclusive global phenomenon, but this need not detract from the central work of Korean and Korean-diasporic participants.

Each of the chapters of this book explores a different arena in and through which contemporary K-pop fans perform deokhu, and in doing so, perform the materialization of affective labor that propels the expansion of the K-pop industry and shapes the personal and collective experiences, meanings, and powers of fandom. Some of these arenas are located firmly within K-pop's neoliberal capitalist industrial structure and contribute to it. In others, fans create practices beyond the boundaries and dictates of these commercial structures by centering fan-specific vantage points and values, which may not always mesh with the profit-centered, consumer values promoted by the industry. Throughout, I supplement traditional research methods of documentation and analysis with a participatory approach, drawing upon my own experiences to illuminate K-pop fandom practices as well the feelings they engender. Feelings are important to consider because affect is so significant in K-pop. Affection, fascination, love, pride, curiosity, and a whole host of other emotions and affective states serve as grounds for K-pop fandom and play key roles in constructing the codes, rules, and values in each fandom. In some ways, this project might be understood as my own felt performance of deokhu—a professional, critical academic work that is also a labor of love for K-pop and its fandoms.

This book begins by focusing on fan practices that are most accessible and require relatively little effort—ones that often accompany or signal new fans' entry into K-pop fandom. These include activities like using smartphones to stream music or vote in competitions. It then proceeds to consider fan activities that require some more effort, and sometimes even courage for fans to put themselves out there in front of their bias and other fans, i.e., creating fan videos. It then moves to fan activities that require even more effort, from organizing fan events to creating an exhibition or publishing a memoir. Toward the end, it considers cases where fans fall out of love with their bias; I explore actions such as exiting the fandom, disposing of the remnants of previous fan activities, and even protesting industry practices or filing a complaint against an idol—all of which are instances of fan labor. While some fans may follow a relatively linear trajectory into and then eventually out of intense fandom, individual deokhu experiences are highly varied, and sometimes even cyclical.

Chapter 1, focusing on the "digital deokhu," examines digital labor in K-pop fandoms. Using ethnographic methodologies, practices of participant-observation, and fan interviews, it explores how the neoliberal capitalist K-pop industry's operative processes utilizing fandom labor (such as streaming, voting, and reorganizing searches) cultivate fan loyalty in conversation with fan desires for liveness and intimacy. Examining fans' digital labor as labor that materializes specific affects among individuals and within communities that form around K-pop fandom allows us to make connections between the technological structures undergirding K-pop fandom and the agential actions of fans whose engagements take place within these structures and also influence their trajectories. Ultimately, digital deokhu practices play a central role in configuring the kinds of attachments and relationships that are possible amid K-pop's online infrastructures of communication and consumption, through which K-pop fandom works to foreground values of authenticity, intimacy, and bonds between fans.

Chapter 2 is about the "video deokhu." It explores recent trends in K-pop fan videos to examine how these productions reflect and mediate relational dynamics in K-pop culture: relationships between fans and idols, fans and the industry, and fandom and society. In particular, this chapter focuses on the following three case studies: first, fan-made videos of virtual autograph signings—also known as video call fansigns—with K-pop idols; second, fan-made videos of opening—also known as unboxing—K-pop albums for the first time; and third, fan-made videos of decorating sleeves for K-pop photo cards. Drawing on my own experiences of attending in-person and virtual fansigns, interviews with fans, and observations of social media posts, I show how across these contexts fans make videos that demonstrate K-pop fandom as an arena of self-making—showcasing one's aesthetics, editing style, and opinions. At the same time, examining this fan-created content that centers fan experiences reveals ways in which deokhu video-makers stage dynamic interactions taking place in fields of power that are being shaped by the content they produce. Through their portrayal of the engagements fans have with idols, other fans, and the industry and its structures, the kinds of videos I examine in this chapter show how fans' affective labor actively mediates myriad aspects of K-pop, including its gender politics and relationship to mass consumerism.

Chapter 3 turns to examine the "archiving deokhu." Here, the focus is on fan practices that originate and circulate beyond the commercial infrastructures of K-pop orchestrated by management companies and other commercial stakeholders. In particular, it emphasizes how fans archive aspects of K-pop music, community, and fandom through documentary formats of photography and writing. Specifically, it examines two types of fan-made products—photography exhibitions and published writings—which together illustrate how the fan labor of documenting K-pop centers fan-specific vantage points and values in the culture of K-pop and its overlapping digital and physical arenas. Within this deokhu archive that exists in relationship to but also exceeds more management-company-driven and commercialized structures, we can see how fans' affective labor materializes individual and communal fan subjectivities that shape the meanings of K-pop's parasocial relationship structures. Contrary to stereotypical accounts of fans that emphasize tropes of brainwashing and exploitation, fans center what their participation in fandom brings to them by creating, documenting, and sharing their own curatorial and narrative portrayals of K-pop fandom through photography and writing: from emotional feelings to insights into their own experiences, to materials for self-transformation, and the making of communal bonds with other fans who participate in the affective worlds they cocreate.

Chapter 4, "The Exiting *Deokhu*," focuses on practices that at first might not obviously appear to be fandom labor, but that I argue should be seen as such. It examines what happens when fans distance themselves from their idols or otherwise choose to stop performing the traditional deokhu role of supporting and promoting the K-pop industry. The deokhu "exit" from fandom, as I explore it, can include a range of behaviors, from gradual forms of disengagement from K-pop fandom to forms of resistive activism performed within the fandom, to high-profile acts of collective mobilization that confront the elements of the industry. When fans mobilize affective labor that they have performed in their deokhu roles to call out misbehaving idols, they provide a particularly compelling site through which to examine even exiting as performing the materialization of affective labor. Especially through mobilizing online to have their voices heard, fans organize and direct their collective affective labor toward undertakings that impact the industry and its performers, notably often focusing their efforts on abuses of power or practices that harm fans. My research shows how the heightened sense of collective agency that emerges from fandom practices, such as all those discussed in earlier chapters, can shape and be shaped by fandom labor directed toward activism that critiques, resists, or demands changes in aspects of K-pop that violate fan expectations and values.

In the epilogue, I consider the legacies of K-pop fandom labor discussed in this book by reassessing my own and others' fan engagements with K-pop. In this massive, ever-growing K-pop fanscape, I see the ongoing legacies of K-pop fan practices as they spill beyond the borders of the neoliberal capitalist industry, working to channel fans' labor of love into an efflorescence of fan activities from collective and communal fan activities to decentralized, personalized labor that represents individual fans' personalities and performances of care.

1 • The Digital *Deokhu*

Online Labor, Parasocial Relations, and the Bonds Between Fans

In April 2016, SECHSKIES, a first-generation K-pop boy group popular in the late 1990s who had disbanded in 2000, reunited. Delighted former fans flocked to DCinside, an online community platform, to discuss how to *jogong*—support—the reunited group. Much to many older fans' surprise, they found themselves completely out of touch with contemporary K-pop fandom activities, which differed from those of their youth. A similar dynamic unfolded two years later, in February 2018, following the reunion of another first-generation K-pop boy group, H.O.T. On H.O.T.'s DCinside fan community, tech-savvy members posted step-by-step guidelines on streaming digital music files and YouTube music videos, commenting on articles, and reorganizing keywords on search engines. Just as SECHSKIES and H.O.T. faced a transformed K-pop landscape vaster than anything their younger selves could have imagined, their fan communities had to navigate a new set of designated codes and rules in K-pop fandom to perform *deokhu*.

In stark contrast to the fan culture norms of previous generations, most of the codes and rules of contemporary K-pop are organized and performed online. And they are done so, moreover, primarily via commercial platforms. These activities are complex and culturally specific, and they have evolved continuously in relation to the neoliberal capitalist South Korean music industry, whose ascent is propelled by the collective efforts of K-pop fans and their evolving relationships with technology, particularly social media but also various new communications apps that straddle the line between personal and communal spaces. In this chapter, I explore the relationship between online practices of K-pop fandom and online technological advancements that structure how fans interact with idols and thereby the wider K-pop entertainment industry that is increasingly dependent on the technologically savvy affective labor that fans perform in digital realms.

Using ethnographic methodologies, practices of participant-observation, and fan interviews, this chapter focuses in particular on the ways the K-pop industry's operative processes of fandom labor—such as streaming, voting, and reorganizing searches—cultivates fan loyalty in ways that negotiate with fan desires for liveness and intimacy. In mainstream social media and communications fan spaces, which are often where fans cultivate their love of K-pop, loyalty is performed primarily through digital engagements that promote and produce profit for the industry. Yet digital labor in K-pop fandoms also, significantly, creates kinship between far-flung fans and facilitates the formation of diverse communities that are more than merely markets.

Using online technology to support their favorite idols, K-pop fans stream and download music, vote for awards, clear searches, and collect materials for idols to use in their navigation of the business. The parasocial relationships developed through digital media and technology, organized around creating opportunities for fans to help idols, motivate fans to participate in such acts of consumption and labor that also encourage other fans to partake in similar unpaid activities that profit the neoliberal capitalist industry. However, it is also the case that fans' digital labor materializes specific emotional affects among individuals and within communities that form around K-pop fandom. This allows us to make connections between the technological structures undergirding K-pop fandom and the agential actions of fans whose engagements take place within these structures and also influence their trajectories. Seen as dynamic exchange with K-pop's online infrastructures of communications and consumption that seek to extract maximum profit in and through fan engagement, digital deokhu practices play a central role in configuring the kinds of attachments and relationships that are possible in K-pop fandom. The digital affective labor performed by fans, as well as the demands this labor sometimes places on stars and the industry to reciprocate attention, injects K-pop's parasocial relationships with pleasurable feelings of authenticity and intimacy that cater to fans' individual and collective desires. It also materializes within K-pop and the wider neoliberal capitalist consumer culture's asymmetrical structures and horizontal social connections among fans who find ways to bond with each other through K-pop.

The Evolution of K-Pop Fandom Labor

Sequential eras of K-pop music and entertainment were accompanied and constituted by changing fandom practices. Examining fandom activities before, during, and after the emergence of many digital technologies allows us to map continuities and ruptures in fandom labor and to theorize the work that the digital deokhu does in producing and maintaining feelings of enjoyment and belonging that are key to K-pop's popularity among its growing legion of fans. More specifically, it also throws into relief Korean fans' pivotal centrality to the wider process of K-pop's meteoric economic growth and globalization, ongoing processes that were and remain propelled not only by the fans' consumer purchases, but also by their enthusiastic adoption and adaptation of new digital social and communications technologies that promoted K-pop nationally and globally.

The first generation of K-pop fandom began with Seo Taiji and Boys in the early 1990s, and evolved with idol acts and groups such as IDOL, H.O.T., SECHSKIES, S.E.S., SHINHWA, FIN.K.L, and G.O.D from the mid to late 1990s. Thus, this was also the beginning of fandom labor. As management companies and artists were developing successful idols, the first generation of K-pop fans were encouraged by fans to support an entire group, even though they might have had a favorite member.

In this pre-digital, pre-internet era, fan support took several forms. Most obviously, there was buying albums. But album sales were tied to a host of other activities that promoted K-pop groups and their music, including fan clubs and weekly TV music programs where viewers called in to vote for their favorite acts. At this time, management agencies were responsible for running fan clubs and fan events. News updates about idols' weekly schedule and fan events were delivered via 152 voice mailboxes, which fans could call to learn information. As the internet spread across South Korea in the late 1990s, official *PC tongshin* (computer network communication enabled via a DOS-based terminal program in the 1990s) fan clubs appeared via Chollian, Hitel, Nownuri, and Unitel. Search engines such as Yahoo! Korea and Lycos Korea became platforms for individual fan pages. These sites, significantly, were founded and operated by fans, who often taught themselves to create pages from scratch or through early website builder templates. They were mainly used for chatting, sharing information, and uploading photos and stories. But also importantly, they imbued K-pop fan culture of the time with certain kinds of affective resonances. The DIY ethos of these sites centered fans as important architects of K-pop culture, while interactive features such as links and message boards cultivated community making between fans.

In the 1990s, experiences of liveness—being copresent in the same time and space—and close proximity with the idols could only be achieved by attending concerts, fan events, and watching weekly TV music programs. Therefore, many fans would be introduced to an idol and be able to form attachments with them only via the mediatized appearance of the idol. Yet internet fan sites offered a platform for deepening these attachments and sharing them with others, potentially in real time—creating a sense of liveness among fans. While K-pop fans became known as *ppasuni*, a term with misogynistic connotations that was often used to describe brainwashed female victims of the capitalist entertainment and music industry, fan activities in support of popular idol groups spread across the nation regardless of the social stigma they elicited among outsiders. Indeed, this stigma could help bring members of this subculture closer together with one another in relationships that were often forged and performed in fan online spaces. Sometimes, especially when fandom was localized in Korea, this could result in physical social gatherings.

First-generation fandom's organized gatherings and strategies laid the groundwork for subsequent practices that would further rely upon digital media and technology. In 2003, the debut of TVXQ marked the rise of the second generation of K-pop. Other groups included SS501, SUPER JUNIOR, BIG BANG, Brown Eyed Girls, Wonder Girls, KARA, FTISLAND, Girls' Generation, SHINee, 2PM, 2NE1, 4Minute, T-ara, f(x), Secret, Highlight (formerly known as Beast), CNBlue, Sistar, Infinite, Miss A, and Girl's Day. With this came the rise of second-generation K-pop fandom, which introduced and revolved around new fan labor practices. This was the era that witnessed the rise of peer-to-peer file-sharing platforms, most famously Napster. In South Korea, digital music files could be shared online via the platform Soribada. Free and pirated downloads were popular ways for fans to acquire and share K-pop in the early 2000s, and it took some time for copyright enforcement in digital spaces to take effect in South Korea. As an activity that both promoted K-pop, but could also potentially cut into the profits of record companies, this form of online labor did not fit neatly into the industry's ideal model of mass consumption. But it did fit into evolving deokhu community norms that emphasized the importance of peer-to-peer exchange, which online file-sharing labor materialized in new forms.

Online fan cafés and fan pages became the major platforms for fan activities, which allowed for diversifying kinds of fandom practices. Much like first-generation fandom, group support was strong; but it was now more acceptable among fans to have a favorite member, or bias, and the proliferation of online fan cafés and pages made it possible to learn more than ever about groups and express support for favorite members. Notably, what had once been mostly fan-operated pages expanded and commercialized, as management companies and other actors sought to monetize ever more nuanced forms of fan engagement. Fans could support their favorite members in official fan cafés, where they could read and respond to messages from the idol, and in Cyworld, a social networking service. Fans could view and comment on the idol's postings in Cyworld's *minihomepy*, a virtual space for individual members. Fans could also leave messages on the visitors' page, and send gifts to the idol's Cyworld account using its virtual currency. As these examples show, fan engagement was more than mere economic exchange, as practices such as message-posting and gift-giving exceed market logics.

In the second generation of K-pop fandom, what has been termed a "support culture" emerged with its corresponding strategies. Eunkyo Kang argues that this is when K-pop fans started "becoming/performing citizens"; that is, when they merged practices of citizenship and social conscience with expressing support and appreciation for groups.[1] This happened alongside the Korean state's own investments in digital development.[2] Building on a longer history of overlap between cultural and political realms, online engagements between K-pop fans allowed for extended and wide-reaching communications to take place, and within this realm, many fans honed their political subjectivities as well as their collective power. Sometimes this support culture mobilized fan labor toward backing idols in disputes with their management companies. In 2010, for instance, three members of TVXQ, one of the most successful idol groups of the second generation, sued their agency, SM Entertainment, claiming the invalidity of the "slave contract" that they had signed as minors. The three left the group and formed JYJ. Despite the court ruling in favor of JYJ, it seems that their former agency pressured the media, blocking JYJ's TV appearances and excluding their music from charts. JYJ fans, as Seung-Ah Lee discusses, "organized both on- and off-line to protect the idols they love and defend their rights as consumers, for example, laboring to place JYJ's album to the second spot on the year's list of best-selling albums."[3] They also, as Lee notes, "initiated a remarkable array of self-policed activities, ranging from publicity campaigns to consumer boycotts, against SM."[4] This watershed moment of fan advocacy in what might otherwise have remained an intra-industry dispute set the stage for future collective mobilizations on behalf of K-pop idols that were sometimes also framed as movements on behalf of the rights of fans themselves.

Some fan support practices that originated or were organized digitally often then extended far beyond online spaces. In support of various causes, fans created advertisements on public transportation and charity events in the idol's name, which were promoted via online fan communities. The first idol advertisements on public transportation were created by fans of JYJ after their legal dispute with SM Entertainment. To cheer on and encourage the idols after the difficult time they had undergone, 9,817 fans raised more than 150,000,000 won in eleven days for bus and subway advertisements. In July 2023, I was able to interview one of the fans who organized the earliest public transportation ads. Her recounting provides insights into how fans understood this labor and its impacts:

> A (FEMALE, 40S): I helped two fellow JYJ fans put up posters celebrating Yoo-chun's birthday in popular areas in Seoul. Other JYJ fans who saw the posters started taking photos and uploading them on internet fan communities. Back then, fans communicated with each other in fan communities created on Daum [a popular search engine that is also the home to numerous online communities called cafés]. After the posters became a topic of interest among fans, there was a consensus that we could promote JYJ further. Managers of JYJ fan communities in Daum cafés got together and divided the work among advertising, design, finance, etc. It was purely a voluntary non-profit fan project. I was in charge of writing press releases. We advertised for fan donations on JYJ internet communities and the fan who was in charge of finances uploaded all the donations and expenses online to make it transparent. I did not expect so many fans to partake in the project. It was right after the legal dispute, and JYJ had just begun starting their activities. Fans' responses were immediate and quick, which made the project thrilling. I came up with the slogan "*Dangsinui cheongchuneul eungwonhamnida* [We cheer on your youth]," which was placed in all of the bus and subway ads. Even though it may seem cliché, I liked how we could send a message that represented the entirety of fans.[5]

This early example of fan support culture illustrates the digital deokhu's use of online spaces and modes of communication to form bonds and project messages in wider local communities. It is important to note that the thrill of this campaign for many fans came from their abilities to oppose what they saw as corrupt industry practices while simultaneously supporting an act. Olga Fedorenko, whose research looks at how fandom ads and fans visiting them make the Seoul Metro social and public in new ways, argues that K-pop idol ads recapture the Seoul Metro from domination by commercial advertisers' interests and appropriate it as a space of fandom, particularly female fandom.[6] In the above example, we might also recognize a message of youth empowerment and solidarity being constructed by fans.

The third generation of K pop fandom emerged in the early 2010s with groups such as EXO, NU'EST, BTS, Red Velvet, SEVENTEEN, Twice, NCT, BLACKPINK, and Wanna One. During this period, orchestration between legacy media and online technologies continued, impacting fan labor practices. *Superstar K*, an annual television talent show first held in 2009, was the first audition TV program. It was followed by *Star Audition: The Great Birth* (2010–13), *I Am a Singer* (2011–16), *Miracle Audition* (2011), *Survival Audition K-Pop Star* (2011–17), and *Produce 101* (2016–present). These programs benefited from technological developments as program viewers voted and expressed their opinions on online platforms. Fan space expanded to personal social networking sites, and support tactics became more complex and diverse. While some of the popular support strategies had evolved from first-generation K-pop fandom, others were new products of digital culture.

The fourth generation of K-pop fandom emerged in the late 2010s with groups such as Stray Kids, ATEEZ, ITZY, TOMORROW X TOGETHER, STAYC, aespa, ENHYPEN, IVE, and NewJeans. While third-generation fandom activities continued, the COVID-19 pandemic created unprecedented challenges for the K-pop industry beginning in early 2020. Fans, idols, and the industry adapted swiftly with online concerts and video call autograph signings. These became the norm until in-person concerts and fan events resumed in Korea and several other countries in late 2021, and often continued in parallel with live events when pandemic restrictions lifted. Since then, management companies have held concerts and fan events in a hybrid format, incorporating both in-person and virtual attendance.

As has been the case for the past three decades, K-pop fan activities continue to swiftly adapt to industry changes and technological innovations, foremost among them the growing primacy of digital arenas of consumption, connection, and exchange. Newly emerging fan activities greatly influence what fans view as their proper role in supporting their favorite idols, the kinds of labor they perform as digital deokhu, and the affective work that this labor does in shaping fan experiences and K-pop's appeal to different audiences. Broadly speaking, looking back over this evolution, it is clear that the growth of digital deokhu practices have raised the potential frequency, expanded the geography, and heightened the emotional intensity of fan engagements. This has been key to the industry's ascending profile and profits, and the industry and other commercial entities that profit from it have developed marketing techniques that cultivate increasingly time- and resource-intensive engagements, eliciting criticism along the way for encouraging addictive behaviors. But it has also given fans wider latitude to shape the affective experiences that K-pop offers them, which can be seen in the ways digital deokhu practices seek to materialize experiences of authenticity and intimacy between fans and idols, and between fans and other fans.

Authenticity and Intimacy in K-Pop Fandom Platforms and Apps

Many K-pop fans today interact with digital media and technology daily. They check their social networks and follow numerous social media accounts dedicated to their favorite idols. Fans will also update their own social media accounts with news about the idol, reposts from other fans' accounts, and the relevant hashtags they add, hoping to increase the idol's brand power.[7] Fans also frequently visit an idol's official webpage and social media accounts to see if the idol has uploaded a posting. Daum Café, Naver Café, Instagram, Threads, TikTok, Twitter/X, V LIVE (which discontinued after merging with Weverse in December 2022), Weverse, and YouTube smartphone apps can be set to notify users as soon as an idol posts. Many idols use such platforms to thank fans when they have received awards, topped charts in music TV programs, or exceeded sales of an album or digital music file. They also reward followers by showing behind-the-scenes footage, selfies, and other forms of spontaneous-appearing content into their daily lives.

All these practices enabled by digital and social media platforms and apps facilitate the affective experience of being copresent with the idol, individually and/or collectively. This can help fans feel that they, either as individuals or as a collective fandom, have the ability to communicate directly with an idol and even the broader industry. Indeed, numerous apps directly facilitate this dynamic. According to the official description of the V LIVE app,

> V is an app that lets you watch the personal broadcasting videos of celebs on your phone. You can follow your favorite celebs, watch their videos, and use comments and "hearts" to share your thoughts and feelings with others. Your activity such as watching videos will affect your "Chemi-beat" for the celeb. . . . As a short form of "chemistry beat," the V team coined the word "Chemi-beat" to express the relationship index between a celeb and you as beat count. Following celebs and watching videos (live or recorded) are ways to increase your "Chemi-beat."[8]

Such acts are important to fans because they set up a two-way dynamic of sending support but also receiving feedback through live broadcasting, comments, and posts. Embedded in the technocratic language of an "index" is a focus on relationality, which relies on dynamics, however asymmetric, of encounter and exchange. This is further underscored by the term *chemistry*, which is typically used to describe spark or compatibility in romantic or other two-way relationships.

Another app in this genre is Bubble, a fan messaging app that emerged in 2019 and has become one of the most popular apps currently available. Fans can subscribe to their favorite idol(s)'s Bubble for a small monthly fee. Idols can send text, photo, video, and voice messages to fans, and fans can reply with text messages. While Bubble's format is akin to group messaging, the app's interface looks like one-on-one chat messaging. This kind of interface can create the illusion of conversing with the idol one-on-one, although fans are aware that numerous other fans are also sending messages to the idol, and that other K-pop industry employees may be monitoring these accounts. Although fans fully acknowledge that Bubble reinforces an "intimacy fantasy," the appearance and felt sense of having a one-on-one conversation with their idol is clearly valued by the digital deokhu.[9]

Significantly, fans do not merely communicate with idols via Bubble—they also communicate with other fans about what transpires on this app. When some fans began to compare the frequency of messages that idols send to fans, social media accounts created by fans dedicated to uploading data on idols' Bubble activities emerged as well. This provided a forum for fans to assess reciprocity. Based on such data, fans were motivated to express ideas about what constitutes desirable digital content or communication from idols, and even move toward developing communal expectations for idol behavior. These can flow from fans' consumer identities and values: some fans believe that it is the idol's rightful duty to send messages frequently, because they had paid for the app's service, and thereby, the idol's service. But there are also expectations that are based on notions of reciprocity for fans' labor that exceed strictly consumerist logics by emphasizing certain cultural and social ideals of relationality. An idol who sends Bubble messages frequently to fans is viewed as a *hyoja* (good son) idol and is complimented for their consistent behavior in communicating with fans about their daily activities and thoughts. On the other hand, idols who are more relaxed in sending Bubble messages are sometimes reprimanded as lacking in fan service and *chosim* (initial commitment) due to their fame and success.

Digital and social media platforms and apps like Bubble are not just a means of communication; they have also become a criteria by which to evaluate an idol's authenticity. The frequency of Bubble messages sent to fans, the variety of messages (whether they are text, photo, video, or voice messages), the content of messages, and the rarity of the content, especially if it contains behind-the-scene photos or previously unknown information about upcoming activities, all become what fans use to measure the idol's authenticity. Here, performances of affective labor from fans are pointed toward materializing affective labor from the idol, who is supposed to do their part to help strengthen the apparent authenticity of fan-idol ties. An idol's affection for his/her fans, as expressed on digital apps, can then further help strengthen the communal ties among fans as the content becomes insider information that fans share with each other. While such informational capital and the influence it may bring within the fandom can certainly become monetized, profit for individuals or the industry is not typically the main motivator of these activities, which are focused on shaping relational dynamics.

Across many of these apps and practices, the use of digital media and technology intensifies the feeling of being copresent with the idol, creating an illusion of intimacy and proximity that facilitates parasocial relationships defined by two-way asymmetric yet mutual attachments. These can help fans become attached to the idol, in an emotional sense, and encourage their participation in fandom activities oriented toward performances of care. This phenomenon began as early as second-generation K-pop fandom with the emergence of earlier versions of social networking sites and intensified during third-generation K-pop fandom as various social networking sites and fandom-associated smartphone apps developed. Over the last three decades, K-pop fans' active use of digital media has changed the traditional role of K-pop fans as audience through fandom activities that often prioritize supporting idols and forming communities with other fans while also setting expectations for reciprocal displays of authenticity and intimacy.

Digital deokhu labor has played an important role in expanding K-pop's global affective reach—that is, K-pop's globe-spanning popularity and the role certain affective states and qualities, particularly authenticity and intimacy, play in propelling this reach and its sociocultural and economic meanings. Sun Jung examines how social media networks affect the circulation of K-pop from a transnational perspective:

> Star-fan dynamics have greatly changed thanks to Twitter, and fans can now closely observe the daily routines of their idols, updated in real time, thus encouraging a strong sense of connection with the stars. . . . Twitter now allows immediate, direct, and constant communication between the stars and their overseas fans. . . . It appears that more and more K-pop stars are communicating with their overseas fans through social media, especially through Twitter. The emergence

> of Twitter has not only changed the dynamics of overseas K-pop fandom, but has also created a new paradigm of transcultural circulation of K-pop.[10]

Jung's idea of social media networks helping idols connect with fans spread out around the globe "in real time" continues to hold importance in K-pop fan studies as the experience of liveness—being copresent with the idol, now often across time-zones and nations—is "central to the process through which fans feel emotionally close to their K-pop idols and this facilitates investment by fans in emotional interactions in real life with other fans" as scholars such as Suk-Young Kim and Rebecca Chiyoko King-O'Riain echo in their research.[11] Notably, fan-based translational and sharing "outreach" labor in digital spaces has often been at the heart of this.

Social media expands fandom's activities and strengthens the fantasy of intimacy, leading to a sense of fans feeling emotionally close to their K-pop idols.[12] This intimacy motivates fans to get involved in fandom activities that require not-insignificant outlays of affective labor.[13] In particular, Michelle Cho explains how Twitter and YouTube helped BTS fans form attachments with the group:

> Across these varied platforms (Twitter, YouTube, VLive, cable, and network television), BTS has delivered a steady stream of "real-life contents" (in the words of the group's leader), inviting fans to engage on an intimate, quotidian basis, and granting a sense of having witnessed the band's personal and professional growth over time. Many fans attribute their intense attachment to BTS to the regularity, frequency, and candor of the group's transmedia contents.[14]

Courtney McLaren and Dal Yong Jin echo Cho's idea that the use of social media is significant in accessing BTS's content and in the fan practices of consuming said content.[15] Similarly, WoongJo Chang and Shin-Eui Park write that ARMY and BTS members' active communication via social media brings forth a "reciprocal, creative, and social intimacy" between them, creating a "special form of emotional exchange, digital intimacy, as traditional boundaries between private and public are breached and reconfigured."[16] Eunjung Kim and Jae-Won Lie argue that it is precisely this kind of intimacy that motivates fans to perform affective labor as they transition from the traditional role of the consumer into creators and intermediaries online.[17]

One can see how the K-pop industry's own engagements with digital media as a way to sell idols as a product can affect how fans regard idols.

Contents that help fans view idols in an intimate way motivate fans to develop parasocial relationships that can be sustained at seemingly ever-increasing numerical discrepancies between the volume of fans and acts. Today, it is not uncommon to see how the "authentic" and "sincere" contents that are uploaded via digital media and technology eventually help strengthen the idol's *seosa* for fans. Literally meaning "narrative" or "story" in the Korean language, seosa can serve as a narrative about the idol's debut, life, or success that could be constructed via media and fandom. And this seosa can motivate fans to perform affective labor to ensure the idol's future success. Most seosa are comprised of a background story that includes overcoming difficulties and hardships, and later maturing into a successful star. The seosa will also complement the idol's personality and attitude toward life and work. Regardless of how true to facts these narratives might be, they can be powerful in eliciting empathy among fans and forging bonds in the fandom. These narratives, which might have been constructed due to media representations and their interpretations by fans, in turn, become motivators for fans to labor for the idol's personal happiness and professional success.

Similar fan activities can also be traced in those of other East Asian contexts, particularly fans of Japanese idols. Patrick Galbraith and Jason G. Karlin examine how female fans of Johnny's idol groups construct individual "coming of age" narratives about their favorite idol members.[18] By doing so, fans feel close to their idol because this narrative creates a kind of "pseudo-intimacy" with the idol, and it is this intimacy that motivates fans to consume further.[19] But in K-pop the narratives that fans construct about their idols tend to center the idea of authenticity and sincerity, which must conform to the idol's actions and personalities in real life as represented in digital form. Heejeh Ahn reminds us that idols' actions and words can be translated as their personality, and because of this, idols are often in a vulnerable position where they are easily criticized.[20] Therefore, idols are compelled to perform emotional labor, for example, having to maintain a bright appearance at all times. By viewing digital content closely and making their own interpretations, fans show affection to idols when the personality revealed in such content matches what they want (or in some cases have decided to be true about the idol), and also condemn them when it does not. The power to approve or condemn, here, can mitigate the felt asymmetry of parasocial attachments.

Sujeong Kim and Sooah Kim explain that for K-pop idol trainees, holding the collective morality of following rules and being humble is especially important.[21] The collectivist ethics of valuing the opinions of others, humility rather than self-confidence, and putting the family and country ahead of oneself still operate strongly in Korean culture and society.[22] This functions as a core principle in idol training. All agencies strictly enforce regulations on smoking, drinking, sexual harassment, etc., and educate idols to be diligent and not cause trouble at school. Kim and Kim state that the reason agencies need high morality and strict character training is not simply because of the importance of traditional values, but because they help make the idol training system sustainable.

> It is not easy for a teen trainee going through puberty to have to train and practice continuously from 6 p.m. to 11 p.m. after school every day for a long period of three to eight years. In order to quell rebellion and anxiety in the face of an uncertain future and to complete the training successfully, adherence to Confucian values, in the form of trusting the agency and following the advice of managers, is required. In addition, in order for young people who become stars before they turn twenty years old to not be arrogant or act recklessly, thereby wasting the money that the agency has invested over the years, agencies prioritize instilling discipline and order. Unlike in the West, where stars are said to symbolize individuality through their unique actions and personalities, in Korea, celebrities gain their stature through their abilities to represent the collective emotions of the people. When a scandal or some unpleasant incident occurs, Western stars are more easily forgiven because they are stars, whereas in Korea, they can easily fall from their star status as they are collectively criticized by the media and the people. In other words, emphasizing character education is related to the company's will and rationality to create long-lasting products without defects. Audiences and especially fans, of course, play a central role in judging whether such efforts are successful.[23]

As Sujeong Kim notes, when an idol's moral personality, such as goodness or sincerity, is revealed, the public instantly praises and rewards them.[24] The emotional egalitarianism and collective moralistic ethos of Korean society sometimes operate as violence, for instance by monitoring every action and word of successful celebrities and demanding adherence to dominant values. However, what is interesting is that fans do not deviate from this public egalitarianism and moralistic ethos. They apply moral standards not only to the idols they don't love, but also to the idols they do love, expecting them to consistently demonstrate authentic morality—which is markedly Korean in nature at time—in numerous regards. In particular, this effect on idols is easily expressed by fandom activities via digital platforms and social media.

Eunkyo Kang argues that the ideas of authenticity and collective moralism do not stop there.[25] They affect the idols' actions after their misdemeanors, for example, how they conduct themselves in the aftermath of missteps or controversies. Kang argues that the phenomenon of idols writing handwritten apologies reflects the moralism of Korean popular culture and intersects with the fandom's distinctive culture of intimacy, which is becoming more and more complex.[26] In the new media era when handwriting is no longer used as a major medium for conveying and preserving information, writing a handwritten apology and photographing it with a smartphone camera and uploading it to social media is meant to represent the idol's sincerity and to appease the angry and disappointed fans. Furthermore, Kang argues that fans' demands for a handwritten apology can also be viewed as a type of consumer feedback movement.

In my interviews, fans testified to how interacting with their favorite idols via digital media and technology helps increase a sense of intimacy and further construct their own version of an idol's seosa, which can become an important motivation for participating in fan activities and performing fan labor.

B (FEMALE, 20S): I feel more intimate with Jungwoo after subscribing to his Bubble, because he tells us what happens in his daily life and sends us photos about it. I thought his texts would be different from the way he speaks, but actually, he texts exactly the way he speaks. So his Bubble helps me understand who he is. I thought he was a shy person, but I learned that he is outgoing and has many friends. I do expect more from him now that I am used to receiving his Bubble messages frequently. I feel lonely when he does not send us anything. When there is an event, I hope that he will send us a selfie. When I see on social media that he was with a friend, I hope he will tell us about it. To do *deokjil* [fan activities], you need to *gwamorip* [to be fully immersed] and seosa can help you gwamorip even more. Jungwoo, who joined NCT later than the other members, received some negative responses at first. But he worked hard, and when he sends us Bubbles about what he did and how he felt that he grew, I also see how much he grew.

C (FEMALE, 20S): Bubble helped me get to know Haechan more because he would send us texts about stuff he does not normally post on his social media account, for example, visiting his parents and what he ate. It helped me construct his character and seosa. He is usually fun and mischievous, but when he sent us Bubble messages while going through a difficult time, I got to know a different side of him. I do expect more from him—I hope he can send us more texts and photos.

D (FEMALE, 20S): After I subscribed to Doyoung's Bubble, I got to know what kind of person he is—he is someone who actively expresses what he is feeling and thinking. I also got to know how much he thinks of his fans. If I did not have his Bubble, I would not have known any of this. After concerts or musicals, I do wish he would text us in detail about how he feels. Because Bubble requires payment, I think it is a platform where fans who really like Doyoung get together so I think it is a platform where Doyoung can express his thoughts more comfortably and easily than other social media platforms. Sometimes I feel proud that Doyoung sends us Bubbles more frequently than other members.

E (FEMALE, 20S): I got to know Jaehyun's silly side after subscribing to his Bubble. I think he feels more comfortable conversing only with his fans via Bubble and can reveal his silliness to us—while the photos on his social media account are very poised and polished, the photos he sends us via Bubble are often blurred or out of focus. He also lets us know about important events in advance. For example, he texted us via Bubble the day before his cover video was released and told us about it.

Of course, this phenomenon is not limited to Bubble—any digital platform can become a ground for idols to interact with their fans.

F (FEMALE, 20S): I got into Hyungwon when I read a reply he posted to a fan's comment on the café. It was such a warm and thoughtful reply. Before I read that reply, I did not know that side of him at all. His replies to fans' posts helped me learn what kind of person he is and construct his character/seosa. And I began to look forward to more of his posts.

As all these interviews show, digital platforms and apps—especially new ones that feature two-way communication between fans and idols, which can then be shared with other fans—play an especially important role in establishing affective bonds, which are made (and made meaningful) through affective labor performed by fans *and* idols in ongoing negotiated proportions and modalities. To be loved, the idol must show the authentic personality and perform intimacy that fans expect. Those who enjoy idol culture might accept and internalize such emotional labor, and even demand it in the form of greater flows of fan service-oriented digital content. In this way, the idol industry turns idols into products that promise happiness by producing and distributing love and closeness, while also setting certain labor expectations for the "authentic" deokhu who is normatively expected to perform constant engagement, which costs time and often money. Throughout this process, labor can be easily elided as such, or rendered intentionally invisible through intersecting industry and fan discourse that centers emotions and notions of service.

Stream, Vote, and Perform Affective Labor Like You Breathe

In early 2019, BTS's management agency HYBE (formerly known as Big Hit Entertainment) credited BTS's global success to fans' streaming practices:

> The company pointed to streaming data and the increase in BTS' physical album sale numbers as verification of how far spread the reach of the group and its fandom is. . . . The rise of streaming has helped many artists from international music scenes, most prominently BTS, gain traction in the States.[27]

Streaming and downloading are the most basic and important tasks for a K-pop fan. According to Wiseapp, five million South Koreans subscribe to Melon, a digital music platform.[28] In addition to Melon, digital music platforms such as Genie, Bugs, FLO, Spotify, and VIBE allow subscribers to stream music on their computers, smartphones, and tablets. Each platform has its own ranking chart, based on the number of people streaming and downloading each song. It is not unusual to see several songs from the same album of a single idol on the chart.[29] Many fans show support for their favorite idols by constantly streaming their music to boost their rankings, a practice known as *summing*, or, *sumseuming*, translated as "streaming music 24/7 as one breathes."

It is easy to dismiss such labor as a consequence of fans who have been brainwashed by the capitalist music industry to do its bidding. But the way in which K-pop fans perform this labor is often strategic, based on careful planning, preparation, and research that reflects their own tastes, interests, and goals. It hints at agency on the part of fans, who master the rules of the industry to use them as they like, as well as the ways the digital deokhu deploys affective labor to materialize strategic engagement from other fans in pursuit of collective goals.

The practice of endless streaming came into being in the age of the digital audio file. With the rise of the digital audio file, as more people subscribed to music streaming sites and CD sales declined, the popularity of digital audio files became far more important for an idol's commercial success. Outlets that measure commercial trends adapted their methods accordingly, moving beyond physical album sales to tabulate digital streams. For example, televised music programs in Korea rely on digital audio files, tabulating them alongside other categories of consumption and assigning them the highest significance in determining the popularity of a song or act. As of August 2024, SBS Medianet's *The Show*, which airs at 6 p.m. on Tuesdays and has been airing since 2011, counted digital audio files for 40 percent, album sales 10 percent, social media for 20 percent, radio appearance for 15 percent, viewer pre-votes for 5 percent, and on-air votes for 10 percent.[30] Pre-voting takes place from Friday at 8 p.m. to Monday at 2 p.m. via the Star Planet app. On-air votes can be cast on the same app during the show. MBC PLUS's *Show Champion*, which airs at 6 p.m. on Wednesdays and has been airing since 2012, counts digital audio files for 35 percent, album sales for 15 percent, global votes for 20 percent, social media for 10 percent, and radio appearance for 20 percent.[31] Global voting takes place from Friday at 8 p.m. to Monday at 2 p.m. via the IDOLCHAMP app. Mnet's *M Countdown*, which airs at 6 p.m. on Thursdays and has been airing since 2004, counts digital audio files for 50 percent, album sales for 15 percent, social media for 10 percent, broadcast score for 10 percent, pre-votes for 15 percent, and on-air votes for 15 percent.[32] Pre-voting takes place from Saturday at 12 a.m. to Monday at 11:59 p.m. via the M Countdown community webpage. On-air votes can be cast on the same website during the show. KBS's *Music Bank*, which airs at 5:05 p.m. on Fridays and has been running since 1998, counts digital audio files for 60 percent, album sales for 5 percent, media appearances for 20 percent, social media for 5 percent, and pre-votes for 10 percent.[33] Pre-voting takes place from Monday at 11 a.m. to Wednesday at 11 a.m. via the Mubeat app. MBC's *Show! Music Core*, which airs at 3:15 p.m. on Saturdays and has been running since 2005, counts digital audio files for 50 percent of the score, album sales for 10 percent, clip views for 10 percent, radio appearances for 10 percent, viewer questionnaires for 5 percent, pre-votes for 5 percent, on-air votes for 10 percent (app votes for 5 percent and text message votes for 5 percent).[34] Pre-voting takes place from Tuesday at 6 p.m. to Thursday at 11 a.m. via the Mubeat app. Viewer questionnaire votes can be cast from Wednesday 9 a.m. to Thursday 11 a.m. On-air votes can be cast either via the Mubeat app or by sending a text message to #0505. Lastly, SBS's *Inkigayo*, which airs at 3:40 p.m. on Sundays and has been running since 1991, counts digital audio files for 55 percent of the score, album sales for 10 percent, social media for 30 percent, broadcast score for 10 percent, pre-votes for 5 percent, and on-air votes for 5 percent.[35] Pre-voting takes place from Monday at 12 a.m. to Saturday at 11:59 p.m. via the Melon app. On-air votes can be cast on the Superstar X app during the show. While this list may feel overwhelming to those uninitiated in the Korean music television scene and its associated digital apps, K-pop fandom is attuned to these criteria and has developed corresponding strategies to optimize the success of the acts they prefer.

One strategy is to encourage more people to listen to an idol's music so that it climbs to the top of the digital music platforms' charts. Many South Korean commuters listen to music. If a consumer has no strong musical preference, he or she may just open a music-streaming app and start listening from the top of the chart. This is one of the main reasons that K-pop fans stream music 24/7. The goal is to have as many people as possible listen to an idol or group's music. Gaining top positions on the digital music platform charts not only racks up points for music TV programs, but also becomes a criterion of an idol's popularity and commercial success, which then assists the idol's management agency in preparing the next album or single. To encourage the management agency to release their idol's new songs and arrange concert tours and fan meetings, K-pop fans work hard to make sure the idol is commercially successful, and they do so in ways that spotlight their own power to make this happen.

K-pop fans research digital music platforms and music TV programs' ranking criteria to find new ways to ensure that all streaming is counted. For example, fans stream a playlist that mixes newly released music and older songs so that the playlist is longer than sixty minutes, because each streaming of a song is counted only once per hour. Sometimes fans will mix music by idols they do not support into the playlist just to make it longer; fans of those idols will reciprocate by doing the same. Fans may lower the volume of the music while it plays, but must make sure that each song plays to the end so that the streaming will be counted. Many fans take the trouble of obtaining unwanted computers, smartphones, and tablets so they can register for accounts and subscriptions to digital music platforms. Because it is difficult to check whether the devices are streaming all day, fans use programs like TeamViewer to connect their devices to their smartphones and monitor their streaming activities. Fans encourage each other by posting FAQs and tutorials for all kinds of devices on blogs, social media networks, and YouTube videos, not only in Korean, but also in English for international fans outside of Korea who do possess a South Korean mobile number and bank account. This linguistic and technological translational labor is important, and mainly provided by multilingual fans who volunteer their language skills for this task, which is widely appreciated. Fans also team up to stream and download on multiple devices. These teams accept email addresses and digital music platform IDs so that they can use such information to register and subscribe to digital music platforms, and stream and download. Because subscriptions for digital music platforms require a monthly fee, these teams accept donations. Donating is a way for fans who do not have other resources—e.g., time, language skills—to participate in this process.

In my interviews, fans testified that they stream their favorite idol's music because they want to support the idol:

G (FEMALE, 20S): I stream because I want my bias to do well. Perks are not the main reason I stream, but it is nice to receive them at fan events. For example, at concerts, some fans will give out one-of-a-kind fan-produced merchandise when you show your streaming counts. I also vote on fan apps because I want my bias to be number one and then we can get his subway advertisement or photo booth frame as a prize.

H (FEMALE, 20S): I stream because it helps the idol's career. And when the album does well, I feel a sense of accomplishment as well.

I (FEMALE, 20S): I stream because I want to see them win first place on TV music programs. If they win first place when I did not stream, it will not feel like we accomplished it together. I stream because I want to win together.

Streaming and downloading not only show fans' support for the idol, but also become a means for fans to prove their own authenticity and loyalty. For example, as the above interview with "G" shows, some fandoms require fans to show their number of streaming counts to be eligible to participate in an event or receive fan merchandise. A Melon subscriber can provide his/her total streaming counts by accessing the Melon app. Melon features functions like certifying streaming activities, writing messages, and encouraging competition between fandoms. In this case, not only a fan's loyalty to a group, but also the incentive that he or she may receive encourages and motivates K-pop fans to continue streaming and downloading.

This practice of streaming music for purposes other than merely listening is not limited to K-pop fans residing in Korea. Qian Zhang and Keith Negus examine how the practices of "data fandom" can greatly influence charts, media and content traffic, and how fans feel a sense of accomplishment via such practices.[36] Meicheng Sun also writes that fan labor beyond Korea is greatly influenced by Korean fans' practices, and shows how such labor becomes a criterion to "distinguish fans from non-fans, and to draw boundaries between the grateful, more enthusiastic fans and the casual self-proclaimed fans who do not contribute to fandom or their idols' success."[37] Some K-pop fans even take a step further in being attentive to and surveilling album sales and chart activities of other musicians. Stephanie Choi explains that these fans will "investigate and report suspicious media manipulation acts to practically secure their fandom."[38]

Fans' streaming is not limited to digital music platforms. Fans also stream music videos from the idol's official YouTube channel and clips from Naver TV (https://tv.naver.com), a popular online platform that provides short clips showing highlights from recent TV programs. Again, K-pop fans research these platforms to come up with ways to ensure each instance of streaming is counted. For example, fans will stream music videos only from the idol's official YouTube channel. Here again, fans must make sure that the music video plays to the end without interruption for the streaming to get counted. Once the music video ends, fans clear the browsing history, delete cookies and data, close the window, open a new one, and repeat the process. In addition to YouTube, streaming clips on Naver TV is important because it helps put the idol in the public eye. Naver is known as "the Google of South Korea," because one-third of the population visits the website every day. More than 130 million queries are conducted daily on the search engine.[39] Naver TV uploads clips, mostly less than five minutes long, which show highlights of popular TV programs that viewers can access on their computers or smartphones for free. While the platform has a category that archives clips by genre or theme, it also has a "Top 100" category for the most popular clips. The clips with high streaming counts appear on the top of the page. Although Naver TV is not a substitute for television, it is influential due to its accessibility and popularity. Thus, Naver TV is an alternative way for fans to showcase the idols that they like. Fans will stream clips of music TV programs and variety shows especially where the idol is received positively. Unlike YouTube music videos, fans do not have to clear the browsing history each time they stream, as repeated viewings are counted. That said, CD bulk-buying (which I will discuss more in chapter 2) continues to be an important activity for K-pop fandoms because album sales continue to be a criterion of an idol's popularity and commercial success.

Voting is another important aspect of K-pop fandom labor. It takes place on weekly music TV programs, in annual music awards, and in competitions among fandoms on apps such as blip, CHOEAEDOL, FAN N STAR, Fan-Plus, Idol Chart, IDOLCHAMP, Mubeat, Mycelebs, Star Planet, StarPlay, and WhosFan, which are community and voting platforms for avid K-pop fans. While such labor can be done within a matter of seconds, voting for annual music awards or competing among fandoms via apps can be more time-consuming and sometimes even costly. Most awards are judged under a set of criteria such as album sales, digital music files, jury votes, and online votes. Online votes can account for as much as 20 to 30 percent of the total score. For the Melon Music Awards (MMA) fans can vote via the Melon app; for Mnet Asian Music Awards (MAMA), fans can vote via Mnet Plus, Spotify, and Twitter. For the Seoul Music Awards, fans can only vote through the organizations' apps. These apps require a certain number of points to cast a vote. To accumulate as many points as possible, fans have to view sponsored ads or make a payment. As with streaming, fans will create several email accounts so that they can vote more than once. The digital deokhu typically shares these strategies for maximizing their voting power with other fans.

This kind of labor of continues throughout the year when fans compete through apps—mainly blip, CHOEAEDOL, FAN N STAR, FanPlus, Idol Chart, IDOLCHAMP, Mubeat, Mycelebs, STAR PLANET, StarPlay, and WhosFan—for incentives such as awards, bus and subway station advertisements, and charity events associated with the idol. Such apps' marketing approaches uses parasocial relationships to encourage competition among fandoms. CHOEAEDOL emphasizes that fans can participate in charity events in the idol's name. While apps serve as a space for organized fan labor, it also becomes a space for fans to communicate with and encourage each other.

Finally, internet support activities require fandom labor in forms such as commenting on articles, engaging with comment threads, and reorganizing search keywords. Fans will post positive comments on a news article associated with the idol and "like" or "recommend" other positive comments so that such comments with the most "likes" will be positioned at the top of the comments. They will also "unlike" or "report" negative comments. Fans will work to ensure that search keywords on search engines, especially Naver, are positive or are closely related to the idol's activities. If there are search keywords that may hurt the idol's image, fans will replace them with positive search keywords. In addition, when fans see negative comments or rumors, they will export them into a PDF and email them to the management agency in preparation for lawsuits. Some management agencies request fans to collect such PDFs and email them to the agency for future lawsuits. This can be seen as an example of how fan labor is materialized by the industry.

One fan I interviewed confided that she clears search keywords that may not only hurt the idol's image, but also the idol's feelings:

J (FEMALE, 20S): I clear search keywords every day because female idols will have nasty keywords next to their names such as "name, body." I do not want my bias to see that when looking herself up on social media so I try to clear them every day.

While streaming and downloading, voting, commenting, reorganizing search keywords, and keeping track of negative comments can be time-consuming, fans view these strategies as necessary to ensure the idol's happiness and success. This set of practices is a recent phenomenon that began around 2015. Fans have decided to take charge of the idol's success by engaging in such labor. Discussing these kinds of practices, Jieun Choe writes,

> As can be seen in the past year, this enthusiastic fandom, especially the "core fans," is not a loose community based on preference, but rather, an association that charges forward together with a common purpose. . . . As the competition in the idol market becomes more intense, so does the fans' will to remove all "bad" external factors for the idol.[40]

Actively engaging in such activities helps to intensify fans' attachment and loyalty to the idol, and elevate the idol's status in the entertainment industry. Fans will make requests via email, fax, and social media networks, and management agencies will take those requests into consideration.

However, as more fans than ever view themselves as active consumers, they can be unreasonable or even hostile, and digital methods of expression and communication can amplify the effects of this kind of behavior. Some fans will cyberbully an idol to express displeasure, for instance, if the idol looks slovenly or gives an unsatisfactory performance. They will also argue with other fans within the same fandom and other fandoms. This sometimes leads to incidents in which some issues—especially pertaining to discriminatory attitudes about gender, race, and sexuality, or the harmful impacts of intrusive surveillance practices—are ignored or silenced "for the greater good." As different goals clash with politics in/among fandoms, those who voice critical opinions about K-pop's relationship to hierarchical or essentialist formations of gender and race, or processes of social marginalization of certain communities (e.g., based on body type or appearance) can be regarded in a negative light.

Significantly, digital deokhu practices cultivated in and through K-pop fandom also spill beyond the borders of entertainment to influence other sectors, notably politics and social movements. Digital fandom labor and its strategies and tactics have wide applications, because fans are other things besides consumers—members of communities, citizens, and social actors. Scholars have recently begun to track how digital strategies developed by fans for supporting idols are sometimes translated by fans into support for political issues or campaigns that are important to them. Scholars such as Wonseok Lee and Grace Kao examined how BTS fans mobilized online to support the Black Lives Matter Movement in 2020, arguing for the fans' potential to enact social change both in and outside of South Korea.[41] As these examples show, interpreting the meaning and politics of the labor of the digital deokhu in K-pop fandom solely through frames of consumerism or industry brainwashing fails to recognize that fans' commitments and interests are multidimensional, with their engagements with K-pop interrelating with other aspects of their lives and worlds.

Conclusion

In this chapter, I have shown how K-pop fandom labor produces and heightens affect and agency through the use of digital media and technology. Through a close examination of K-pop fans' activities via social networking sites, digital music platforms, fandom-associated apps, and voting apps, this research explains how K-pop fandom labor has changed with the evolution of the Korean music industry since the 1990s. Over this period, fans have developed corresponding strategies for working together to materialize their desires and desired outcomes, hinting at evolving forms of agency on the part of such fans, who master and take advantage of the rules of the industry and its communications and promotional infrastructures. While media accounts and even many scholarly ones dismiss such fandom labor as unproductive or even obsessive, this research argues that K-pop fans fully understand the Korean music industry system and possess their own complex reasons for performing deokhu as they do. Their acts of digital fandom labor are deliberate and strategic, orchestrated to produce particular affects that fans desire and forms of collectivity and community building that allow them to amplify the visibility and efficacy of their efforts.

Especially with evolutions in digital technologies, K-pop fandom has become a highly organized networked community with specific communal goals that can be discussed and adapted at rapid speeds and across global spaces. Fans will mobilize their resources via digital media and technology and perform affective labor to achieve those goals. Built on affective constructs such as romantic versions of parasocial relationships and attachments to an idol characterized by asymmetric yet essential forms of two-way exchange and nuanced codes of conduct, fandom practices and technological developments influence each other. While digital media and technology facilitate collective experience, the power of technology can shift to the fandom, as fandom's fervent mobilizations motivate digital media and technology to develop more cutting-edge resources and services that cater to fans' priorities.

Unlike first-generation fandom in which fan clubs had top-down policies, fans today have worked to construct more horizontal relationships when working together, while the multimodal networks of social media networks and smartphone apps create "imagined communities" that mediate relational dynamics in K-pop fan culture. It is becoming increasingly unproductive to discuss K-pop in isolation from its fandom, because an idol cannot become popular without fans' labor, which is often digital labor. In this sense, K-pop idols and music are not the only things being exported and circulating globally; so are digital deokhu practices and associated expectations for fans *and* idols *and* the industry that they cocreate. K-pop fandoms are self-reflexive, constantly reevaluating their activities and modifying them to be more efficient and productive. K-pop fandom's goals are clearly defined and specific—the idol's happiness and success, which is often understood as being in relation to the happiness and success of fans, which is stoked by feelings of authenticity and intimacy in parasocial relations and horizontal fan relationships. At the same time, this kind of phenomenon shows how the industry leads fans into believing that they are responsible for the idol's success. This responsibility leads to greater attention among fans to archiving K-pop, creating spaces for critical reflection on fandom, and steering industry norms, including idol behavior, as will be discussed in the following chapters.

2 • The Video *Deokhu*

Mediating Selfhood and Relations of Power Through Fan Videos

In January 2021, Korean comedian Gang Yu-mi created a YouTube clip that parodies an idol fansign ("autograph signing"), which went viral among K-pop fans.[1] In the clip, Gang depicts a virtual interaction between an imaginary male idol named Gang Min and his Korean female fan, playing both roles. Sitting in a room decorated with balloons, the nervous fan tells her friend that she went to a salon to get her hair done, carefully selected her wardrobe, and prepared gifts in anticipation of the fansign. But when the video call happens, the idol shares nothing of her effort or enthusiasm. To his fan's excited conversation, Gang Min merely repeats "Oh, really?" in a monotone voice, wearing a blank expression.

Gang Yu-mi's clip went viral for several reasons. Its representation of the male idol offers critical commentary on idols who display a lethargic and inattentive attitude in performing "fan service," a phenomenon that elicits strong emotions among invested fans, who, as we have seen in the previous chapter, tend to expect expressions of authenticity and intimacy. Although Gang's clip represents a fictional situation, many viewers posted comments expressing that the male idol's inattentive attitude is unforgivable because it is the idol's "code of conduct" or "duty" to perform a specific kind of fan service. In addition, the humorous clip became viral because numerous K-pop fans understood and sympathized with the ways in which it captures and parodies the role of affective labor (or lack thereof) in the idol-fan dynamic. The clip's popularity and the discussion it provoked reveal the extent to which K-pop fans and viewers are aware of how relationships of power, demonstrated through asymmetric performances of affective labor, inflect fan and idol performances in the K-pop industry. This comes to the fore particularly strongly in fan-made videos, which represent a key site where fans not only perform *deokhu*, but also use these performances to shape K-pop's dynamics and meanings.

K-pop fans have long made videos on social media platforms, where they can be seen performing deokhu identity through a variety of visual practices grounded in affective labor. Of course, the growing accessibility and technological sophistication of digital devices with high-quality cameras has contributed to this pattern, but so have other factors. The practice of fan video-making dramatically increased during the COVID-19 pandemic, providing a space for global fans to engage with idols and with each other virtually. This chapter explores recent popular trends in K-pop fan videos to examine how these productions reflect and mediate relational dynamics in K-pop culture: relationships between fans and idols, fans and the industry, and fandom and society. In fan-made videos, I argue, deokhu performances reveal a shift in focus from centering the idols to centering the fans themselves. Through the affective labor of performing fan identity, fans construct representations of themselves while also helping to shape norms and expectations around what constitutes desirable relational dynamics in K-pop. In videos and video performance especially, the gendered dynamics of the workings of affective labor in K-pop and fandom come to the fore, in part, I argue, because they are being made visible as such by fans themselves, who engage in various ways with relations of power in K-pop through practices of video-making that center fans.

In particular, this chapter focuses on three case studies: first, fan-made videos of virtual autograph signings—also known as video call fansigns—with K-pop idols; second, fan-made videos of opening—also known as unboxing—K-pop albums for the first time; and third, fan-made videos of decorating sleeves for K-pop photo cards. Drawing on my own experiences of attending in-person and virtual fansigns, interviews with fans, and observations of social media posts, I show how, across these contexts, fans make videos that demonstrate K-pop fandom as an arena of self-making. By this, I mean that fan videos, in both content (such as their aesthetics and the opinions they express) and form (such as in their editing style and where and how they are posted), seek to communicate information about the fans themselves, and particularly their own fan personas, perspectives, or values. At the same time, examining this fan-created content that centers fan experiences reveals ways in which deokhu video-makers stage dynamic interactions taking place in fields of power, which video-makers also attempt to shape and sometimes reshape. Through the interactions they depict fans having with idols, other fans, and the industry and its structures, the kinds of videos I examine in this chapter show how fans' affective labor performed in and through video-making and video engagement actively mediates myriad aspects of K-pop, especially its gender politics and relationship to neoliberal capitalist consumerism.

Fan-Made Videos of K-Pop Fansigns

Autograph signings, or "fansigns," are a unique opportunity for fans to meet a K-pop idol one-on-one. These events are organized by the idol's management agency in cooperation with a retail company that is promoting the idol's new album or product. Although each fan has no more than a few minutes to converse with the idol, other fans can observe the interaction, either in-person, or (as we will discuss) via fan-made videos, depending on the event. In addition to meeting an idol, fans can meet each other and form communities at these events and in the discussions that happen around them later. Many fans post testimonies on social media describing what it had been like to meet their idol. As these posts go viral, fansigns become a source of entertainment for fans and a promotional opportunity for the idols. For some fans who continue to attend fansigns several times, their testimonies on social media serve as a criterion in being a "named," or well-known, fan in the fandom. When the COVID-19 pandemic struck in early 2020, numerous K-pop concerts and fan events were canceled and moved online. Virtual fansigns, also known as "fan video calls," flourished in these virtual spaces. This fostered the proliferation of fan-made videos of fansigns, which allow for expanded viewing of and participation in these events.

Although the history of fansigns in K-pop fan culture dates back to the 1990s, few works have examined fansigns and their impact on K-pop fan culture.[2] Relatedly, a small number of scholars have examined the impact of fan videos in K-pop fandom and the industry.[3] Some of the most popular fan videos are K-pop cover dance videos on YouTube. Chuyun Oh examines K-pop fans' cover dance videos on YouTube and looks at how they perform cultural exchange on the internet that "reshapes the diffusion of dance styles and ideas":

> During this process, dancing—dance education, presentation, and reception—is mediated by and for social media space and audiences online. Yet, this mediatization is as physical as it is virtual. By flawlessly adapting and embodying K-pop song lyrics, facial expressions, gendered choreographies, makeup, fashion, and fandom culture, they create an alternative space of performing linguistic, ethnic, gender, racial, and cultural identity—a Thirdspace of practicing, performing, and redistributing dance in between and across dance studio and smartphone, theater and YouTube, reality and virtuality, and being themselves and being like K-pop idols, individually and collectively.[4]

As another prominent genre of fan-produced video media, fansign videos also offer important insights into fandom culture and labor. Using ethnographic methodologies, I explain and analyze this phenomenon more closely because, I argue, fansigns have become an important and highly visible realm for fans to represent themselves and interact with idols, the industry, and other fans. As fan-produced videos of these events circulate beyond their immediate participants, they shape the broader economy and culture of K-pop in key ways. The combination of collective moralism in Korean society, fans' consumerist attitudes, and the recent popularity of short-video culture has accelerated the trend of fan videos including moments of fans requesting or even demanding that idol perform *aegyo* ("attitude or behavior of appearing cute to others," meaning cuteness). Thus, fansign videos allow us to better understand how the performing video deokhu works to actively shape affective entanglements between fans and idols that are deeply enmeshed in broader social and economic systems yet also show responsiveness to fans' creative labors.

Information on when and where a fansign will take place is announced and posted on the idol's fan club, social media account, and vendor's website. Also posted are the guidelines on entering the drawing by which fans will be selected to participate: the deadline, where and how to buy albums, the number of fans to be selected (which is different by event, ranging from 10 to 200), and when the winners will be announced. My own long-running experience with fansign events provides concrete details. Prior to the pandemic, when I wanted to enter a drawing, I would go to a designated retail store, tell the salesperson that I would like to enter the idol's fansign, and purchase albums that would make me eligible. After accepting my payment, the store would give me a receipt confirming the number of albums I had purchased to enter the drawing. Some stores would give me a ticket for each entry. I would write down my contact information and place the tickets in a designated box. Fans residing outside of Korea could enter the drawing by purchasing albums online. A day or two after the entry deadline, the list of fans selected from the drawing would be announced on the retail company's website. The company would also post information about the fansign—for example, instructions that fans are to enter the fansign venue at a designated time, usually an hour or two before it begins, and bring an ID. Many fansigns prohibited fans from bringing food or gifts; some allowed this. Of course, it is always prohibited for a fan to do anything that might harm the idol. During the COVID-19 pandemic, some elements of these protocols were updated in accordance with the move to virtual spaces. Today, fansigns still occur in-person but are often virtual.

When a fansign starts, the staff guides fans to line up, and then guides each individual fan to the idol. During the encounter, the staff keeps track of time; each interaction lasts two to five minutes. When the time is up, the staff requests that the fan end the conversation so the next fan can be introduced. While this brief encounter with an idol may not seem worth all the trouble involved in attending, fansigns are one of the most—if not *the* most—coveted K-pop fan events. In addition to meeting the idol personally, this event allows fans to observe the idol walking into the venue, sitting in his seat, waving to the crowd, drinking beverages between signing albums, and conversing with fans. Many fans bring cameras to photograph these candid moments. At fansigns, fans also meet with each other and form friendships. Before and after fansigns, I have met up with other fans with whom I had been communicating on social media. Some fans even became *deokmates*—close friends who keep each other updated on the idol's activities and go to events together.

Venues are important factors in creating the fansign experience. Some fansigns are held in public places like shopping malls. At these events, many fans who had not entered or won the drawing can still watch from afar. These events tend to be very noisy as fans shout to get the idol's attention. I remember that some of the fansigns in shopping malls were so loud that I had to raise my voice when speaking to the idol and he had to lean forward to hear me. These are not the best circumstances for a conversation with an idol. Perhaps for these reasons, many fansigns are held in private venues. Those fansigns, in my experience, have been much more enjoyable. And because the idol's fans tend not to shout at him, all I could hear during the event was the clicking of fans' cameras and occasional oohs and aahs. Whereas management companies might prefer that these events be staged spectacularly in publicly traversed centers of consumption like malls, the general trend, likely reflecting fan preferences, has been toward more intimate venues where conversational connection can be emphasized (and indeed, videoed).

Notably, K-pop companies and fansign vendors impose strict rules before and during the fansign, many of which target recording devices. Although many fans find some of these unreasonable, they rarely voice their opinions to the companies and vendors directly, because they are afraid that in doing so, they will be blacklisted and will not have a chance to enter or be selected for fan events in the future. In such situations, one can see how much companies and vendors hold power over fans—affective laborers who are not only consumers, but also content creators and distributors who help the companies and vendors profit—and how fans have no choice but to succumb to their rules if they want to continue participating in the events without restrictions. This does not mean, however, that fans merely accept these circumstances and do not work to devise ways to critique or change them.

For example, on July 8, 2023, several fans of the boy group &Team posted on social media calling out the group's management for checking fans' bodies and underwear to search for hidden recording devices.[5] Fans posted that they were confused and felt as if they were sexually harassed. When fans purchase albums and apply for fansigns, they are required to agree to the vendor's regulations and cooperate with the staff during the event. But staff touching fans' bodies and demanding them to take their clothes off to prove there were no hidden recording devices turned out to be a step too far. But there are no testimonies that any fan, angered by such treatment, left the fan event, even in an unpleasant situation such as this. Instead, every fan complied with the vendor's demands and regulations, even though they felt deeply mistreated. Presumably in response to immediate complaints, HYBE's fan commerce media platform Weverse Shop posted a statement the next day explaining that while fans have cooperated with the company's guidelines in previous fan events, there were many fans who had hidden recording devices and it was necessary for the female staff to perform a body check. While Weverse Shop apologized for making fans uncomfortable, they received much criticism from fans as the company used the English term *body check* in the statement instead of the Korean term *momsusaek*, which denotes conducting a body search, as if to lift some of the responsibility off their shoulders. The statement also did not mention that the staff checked the fans' underwear and that the fans felt they were sexually harassed—something that some fans pointed out in online discussions. While the possibility of fan recordings was deemed somehow potentially harmful, the actual harm inflicted by invasive body checks was written off. This incident shows how fans, even as they are recognized as important to K-pop's global popularity, are often subject to the companies' and industry's strict guidelines and mistreatment. Additionally, there is the irony of management companies exerting invasive control over fans' bodies to check for recording devices, when fan-made media of these events play such an important role in promoting them and the idols. Fans recognize this irony, and commented upon it.

To enter a virtual fansign, fans must purchase albums online, and fans who win the drawing will meet with the idol on a video call platform such as KakaoTalk, LINE, or WeChat. K-pop management agencies will also cooperate with foreign vendors for virtual fansigns. While each vendor will have its own platform and guidelines, I have observed and experienced firsthand how Chinese vendors such as Owhat and Yizhiyu previously showed the ranking of the top ten fans who purchased the most albums in real time. This kind of chart will motivate fans to purchase more albums to be selected for the fansign. For several fansigns, I observed and experienced that fans will wait and then rush to purchase more albums right before the entry closes, based on the ranking information. The new norm of virtual fansigns has been accompanied by fans documenting these encounters and uploading them for others to see. Often, these are screen recordings, usually edited by the fan, and they may be shared on social media afterward.

Fansign Experiences with Jiwon and Lucas, 2017–2021

To examine fansigns, I combined research derived from interviews and social media with my own experiences attending approximately twenty-one in-person and virtual fansigns from 2017 to 2021—fourteen fansigns of first-generation K-pop idol Eun Jiwon of SECHSKIES and seven fansigns of third-generation K-pop idol Lucas, a former member of NCT and WayV. In eleven cases, I created videos of these encounters, editing the screen recordings and sharing them via Twitter/X. These concrete examples provide useful insight into the more complex individual dynamics of fansign events as well as the ways videos of individual fansigns, produced through fan labor, become circulating texts that contribute to larger processes of meaning-making about K-pop.

I have been a fan of K-pop star Eun Jiwon since 1997. When I was in middle school and high school, I did not have the opportunity to attend fansigns. Although I attended his concerts, my seat was miles away from the stage, and Jiwon was no bigger than my fingernail. I was curious about what he would be like up close. How different would he look and sound? How tall would he be?

An opportunity to meet Jiwon came when I was residing in South Korea from 2017 to 2019. In April 2016, Jiwon's group, SECHSKIES, had reunited sixteen years after disbanding in 2000. The release of a new album brings many opportunities for fans to meet their idols. In fall 2017, SECHSKIES released their fifth full-length album, *Another Light,* and their nationwide tour from December 2017 to January 2018 took them to Seoul, then Gwangju, Goyang, Busan, and Daegu. There were also five fansigns in October and November 2017, four of which I attended. Because I only had a few minutes to talk to him, I always prepared a short speech or talking points. I mostly talked about how much I enjoyed the new album and how much I was looking forward to the upcoming concerts. I also wrote letters and brought gifts.

I had assumed that meeting Jiwon once would be enough. But to my surprise, seeing my favorite idol up close, and having a conversation with him, made me want to see him again. The memories from the fansigns became a constant source of happiness and encouragement, and—similar to experiences recounted by memoirs that will be discussed in chapter 3—those moments helped me to get through the day, work harder, and transform myself. For me, this in part meant working on my research, which would allow me to spend more time developing academic work on K-pop. And I became determined to enter more fansigns and meet Jiwon again.

Although some people believe that the relationship between fans and idols is superficial, I contend that there is a special sense of community and sincerity that binds fans to their idols, and this bind can be made or made stronger through chances for one-on-one interaction, which can be participated in vicariously by others through video-making. What makes that sense of community and sincerity real are the efforts of both the fans and idols, and these can be seen at fansign events. For example, I have seen Jiwon focusing intently on each fan, looking into her eyes, and expressing his thoughts, giving the impression that he truly appreciated and respected each fan. Although Jiwon's words are simple and short, they convey sincerity, which I noted in my own encounters with him. At a fansign held on Jiwon's birthday, June 8, 2018, I told him how thankful I was to have been his fan for more than twenty years and how much I appreciated his hard work in the highly competitive entertainment industry. Jiwon thanked me and wrote "Let's see each other for a long, long time" below his autograph.

At the March 16, 2019, fansign, when I told Jiwon that I had been offered a professor position in China, he seemed genuinely happy and congratulated me. He gave me a thumbs-up and wrote "Your hard work paid off! So proud of you, Areum" under his autograph.

At the virtual fansign on December 20, 2020, I talked about my difficulties during the pandemic and how Jiwon's music and TV programs gave me positive energy to cope with them. After listening intently, Jiwon agreed that many people were becoming depressed during the pandemic and wrote "You are such a bright person. That's so good to see!" below his autograph.

A different sense of community emerges when the idol recognizes a fan that he has met several times. Jiwon eventually started to recognize me. To my surprise, at the March 16, 2019, fansign, Jiwon greeted me with "We meet again!" "Do you remember me?" I asked. "Of course, I do. Even though I can't remember your name, when I see your face, I recognize you," he answered. At the July 5, 2019, fansign, Jiwon greeted me with "I keep forgetting names, but when I see your face, I recognize you. We've met many times

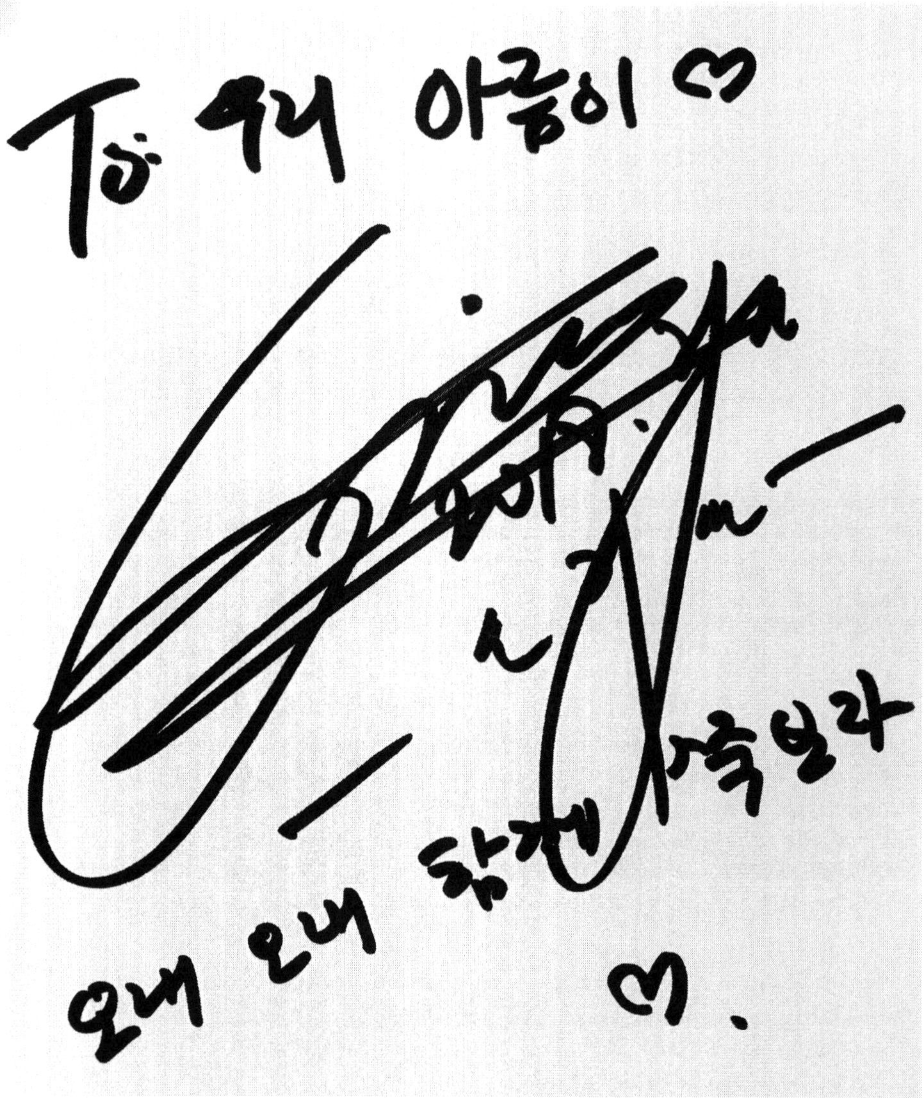

Figure 5. Eun Jiwon's autograph. Photo by Areum Jeong.

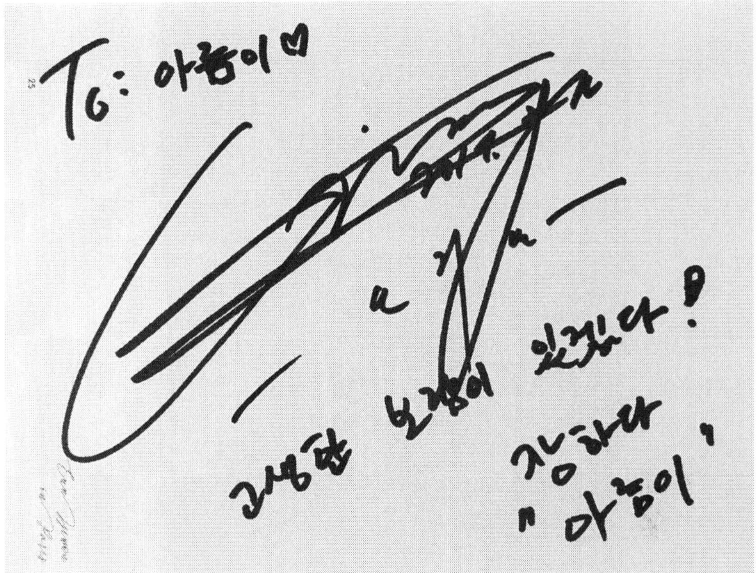

Figure 6. Eun Jiwon's autograph. Photo by Areum Jeong.

before." And at the December 20, 2020, virtual fansign, which was the first virtual fansign since the COVID-19 pandemic, Jiwon asked "How have you been?" when he saw my face on the screen. Because I had never expected him to remember me, I was always surprised when he did. At those times, I believed that my efforts were paying off, even though I had never sought his recognition. When I showed videos of my encounters to friends, several commented that I had become an authentic, loyal fan because he remembered me. This made me feel appreciated and continues to inform how I view fansign events' potential to provide recognition for the affective labor and material investments of fans.

In 2021, when the COVID-19 pandemic had put a stop to all in-person K-pop fan events, I participated in seven video calls with NCT/WayV's former member Lucas—January 15 for NCT's *Resonance Pt. 2* album promotion, and April 15, 24, 29, and May 7, 14, and 25 for WayV's *Kick Back* album promotion. Among these seven fansigns, two were organized by Korean vendors, Interpark and MK Media, and five were organized by the Chinese vendors Owhat and Yizhiyu.

After the list of fans selected for the drawing was announced via the vendor's app and Weibo account, I received a text message requesting my personal information and containing guidelines for the video call:

> The staff will call you first for identification check. Please show us your ID card (or passport, alien registration card) when you pick up the phone call. . . . If your internet does not work you can ask us to stop. However, the time spent on call will be included in the total time. . . . If you fail to answer the phone call three times, your call will be canceled. . . . The staff will remind you at 1:30, and ask you to hang up at two minutes. (Yizhiyu, January 25, 2021, translated from Mandarin to English)

> You are the Nth person in the Lucas online video signing. . . . Each winner must reserve time to be online and wait for the video call connection when the network is very good. Each winner has only one video opportunity and can't repeat the video call. The same candidate cannot be repeated through different accounts. Violators will be denied a call by the staff. (Owhat, April 22, 2021, translated from Mandarin to English)

To conduct the fan event in an orderly fashion, K-pop management companies and fansign vendors request fans to abide by every rule that they had been notified of before the event. Numerous fans post their experiences on social media about how the employees running the event would strictly adhere to the rules without considering case-by-case situations. For example, some fans had technical difficulties and were not able to converse with the idol, but were not offered help after the second video call. This can lead to fans feeling unappreciated by management companies, but among other fans, someone shut out of an event due to technical difficulties will usually receive sympathy or commiseration. There is clearly an ongoing dialogue between how management companies interpret fairness (usually, things being the same for everyone from a top-down perspective) and what fans themselves deem to be fair (often some attention to individual circumstances so as to allow all participants equal time to connect with idols).

On January 15, 2021, I had my first video call with Lucas, for two minutes and sixteen seconds. When the Yizhiyu staffer called me, I immediately showed her my ID. After verifying it, she told me to wait. I could not see anything, as the staffer had covered the screen with a piece of paper, but I could faintly hear another fan talking to Lucas. This meant that the organizers had prepared several mobile phones and were lining up the fans to save time between calls. After a minute, the voices subsided and the staff member removed the piece of paper. Suddenly, Lucas appeared on the screen. He was wearing a white sweatshirt and had ash-pink colored hair that sometimes looked lavender depending on the lighting. Because it was my first call with Lucas, I felt very nervous even though I had prepared talking points. I think Lucas felt shy as well, but he paid close attention to what I said and was very responsive. During our short conversation, I briefly introduced myself and explained how and when I became interested in NCT/WayV and Lucas. When I told Lucas that he cheered me up on days I missed my family in Korea, Lucas replied that he also had not visited his own family in Hong Kong for a long time and encouraged me to cheer up. When I asked him when he would visit Chengdu again, he replied enthusiastically that he loves Chengdu and asked me some questions about myself and my work in China. Two minutes went by in a flash. Lucas smiled brightly and raised his arms to create a heart over his head, exclaiming "Wo ai ni! (I love you!)" as the staff ended the video call.

Three months later, on April 15, 2021, I had my second video call with Lucas, which lasted an even two minutes. I still felt awkward and shy, and I do not think Lucas remembered conversing with me in January. I did not expect him to, due to his busy schedule and the vast number of fans he converses with during multiple fansigns. We chatted about the new *Kick Back* album and his upcoming activities when the MK Media staff ended the call abruptly at 1 minute and 59 seconds without any warning. Although I was aware that each fan had two minutes to converse with Lucas and that the staff must follow the rules, it felt unpleasant that the staff did not even allow a few seconds to wrap up the call.

On April 24, 2021, I had a video call with Lucas that lasted 3 minutes and 48 seconds. My third video call, which was organized by Owhat, was longer than the previous two video calls because there were technical issues. During all of the first minute, Lucas's screen was not functioning properly. "I can hear you, but I can't see you," he kept saying in a worried tone. "What should we do?" he asked looking at the staff member to his side. The staffer might have signaled him to end the call for now and try again later, but at that moment, the screen must have cleared up, because Lucas smiled and said "It's working, it's working!" while holding up an "OK" gesture with his left hand. Panicked that I had lost precious time due to technical difficulties, I frantically said, "We're starting now, OK? We're starting now!" Because it was my third call with Lucas, I felt less nervous, and Lucas, who said that he remembered me, also seemed more comfortable than before. I asked how his day was and we chatted about his recent activities. When I asked what he would say to his pet beagle Bella when he returned to Korea, Lucas held out his arms and said, "Bella, come to Dad!" I laughed. "I'm Bella's Dad," he said proudly, with a bright smile. Two and a half minutes passed by, and Lucas, smiling brightly with his arms raised over his head to create a heart, said, "See you again!" When I edited my conversation with Lucas and posted it on my social media account, thousands of fans responded and shared Lucas's affection for his pet.

On April 29, 2021, my fourth video call, organized by Interpark, lasted 3 minutes and 30 seconds. I felt even less nervous than I was on the previous call. When Lucas saw me, he smiled brightly and waved. "How have you been?" he asked. It was evident that he remembered me. When I asked how he was, he replied, "I'm a bit busy, but I think of you guys every day so I'm OK!" When I told him that I was studying Mandarin so I could watch his activities without subtitles, he looked impressed. Then he smiled slyly and asked me something in Mandarin quickly. My mind suddenly went blank. When I wailed "Ting bu dong! [I can't understand what you are saying!]" Lucas laughed so hard his body rocked back and forth. "But I think you can do it, *nuna*," he said, encouraging me to study harder. I knew there was not much time left, so I asked my last question: "Lucas, what makes you happy these days?" For several seconds, Lucas pressed his lips together without saying anything. Then he answered earnestly: "Honestly, fansigns or when I meet fans during my schedule, because it has been a long time since I saw my fans." He enunciated each word carefully and slowly. When I posted this conversation on my social media account, numerous fans responded and shared their pleasure at how much he cared for his fans.

On May 7, 2021, I had a video call with Lucas for 2 minutes and 29 seconds. I could tell that he felt even more comfortable with me because he leaned very close to the screen compared to the first two video calls. We chatted about his recent activities and encouraged each other to persevere during the pandemic. At the end of the call, he created a small heart with his fingers that he held close to his face and said "I love you!" in Korean, then waved goodbye.

On May 14, 2021, I had a video call with Lucas for 3 minutes and 6 seconds. As soon as he saw me, he greeted me with a big smile and his usual "How have you been?" I told him I had good news and bad news and asked what he would like to hear first. After a few seconds, he said, "Bad news first!" I told him since this might be the final fansign for the *Kick Back* album promotion, I would not be able to see him for a while, but would await the new WayV album. Lucas laughed, rocking his body back and forth. "Now, good news!" I told him that I was going to teach a K-pop course in the fall semester and held up the course flyer. "I plan to include NCT songs, of course!" Lucas's eyes grew big and he smiled when he saw that I had inserted his photo in the course flyer. "I really wish we could meet in China," Lucas said. "In-

Figure 7. Lucas taking a photo during a video call with me. Screenshot by Areum Jeong.

person concerts and fan meetings have resumed! If WayV is able to have a concert or fan meeting in China, I can go see you perform!" I said. "I'm going to try really hard to make that happen!" said Lucas, holding out his fist as if to fist bump. "I want to show you our stage!" As the call came to an end, he waved and then raised his arms to create a heart over his head. "See you again next time for sure!"

On May 25, 2021, my seventh and final video call with Lucas lasted 3 minutes and 39 seconds. Because this was going to be the final fansign for the *Kick Back* album promotion, I had prepared a handwritten letter for him which I slowly read out loud for a full minute so he could understand every word. I had contemplated whether I should spend a full minute out of my three-minute conversation to read the letter, when attending this fan event was quite costly. While I was reading out my letter, I could not see Lucas's expression, but when I watched the recording after the fansign, I saw that he had listened attentively to every word with a serious expression, nodding many times. When I finished reading the letter, I suddenly felt very self-conscious and shy and covered my face with the letter. Lucas laughed as he clapped his hands. Then he sat up straight and said, "Wow, thank you so much. Areum *nuna*, you were really the most memorable fan during the *Kick Back* fansigns. Your words always encourage me, so I truly thank you. Lucas will make better performances, and on better stages, and we can cheer for each other and go high together!" Before the call ended, I made my first and final request, which was to take a selfie with him, albeit virtually. Lucas readily agreed and reached for his own mobile phone. Holding his own phone up high in the air, Lucas turned so I could see the back of his head and leaned closer to the screen. He took the selfie and showed me the photo. The staff called out that the time was up. "See you again next time! Bye! Fighting!" Lucas exclaimed as he waved goodbye.

"*Aegyo*, Please": The Neoliberal Capitalist, Consumerist, and Gendered Culture of Fansigns

While attending fansigns and viewing those of others, including through fan videos, I was able to observe, as a co-performer witness, how fansign events reveal, but also provide a ground for, the mediation of the neoliberal capitalist layers of the K-pop industry, the consumerist fan culture, and its gendered politics. These qualities of K-pop can be seen in the high costs to attend fansigns and the physical detritus they produce, in the potentially hierarchical social dynamics among fans they can structure, and in the attitudes toward the fields of affective labor they can inculcate. But as fans perform deokhu identity through video-making and engagement, their affective labor opens space for reflecting upon K-pop's relationships of power, both for consumers of these videos, and for scholars.

It is important to foreground the material investments fansigns require. Again, my own experiences provide concrete insights. Because I wanted to improve my chances of being selected for each fansign, I usually purchased tens or sometimes hundreds of copies of the same album depending on the idol's popularity and competitiveness of the event. Buying large quantities of albums for fansigns is a problematic issue in the K-pop industry, as the industry does not engage much with the negative consequences for individual fans and the environment. Many fans of popular idols purchase hundreds of albums to ensure their place in a fansign. There is practically no chance of being selected for fansigns by purchasing one or two albums. The more albums someone buys, the better the chances of being selected. Thus, many fans try to speculate what the "fansign cut"—the fewest albums to purchase and still be selected—is. In order to try to keep fans from spending more than minimally necessary, fans also share information on the retail companies' selection policies. For example, Company X might select 80 percent of winners from customers who purchased the most albums and 20 percent of winners by random drawings. Company Y might select 90 percent from those who purchased the most. Company Z might purposefully reject fans who attended the previous fansign, even if they purchased many albums in the next round. But none of the information above is stated in guidelines by K-pop management companies or fansign vendors. Such information mostly travels by word of mouth among fans. Some third-party sellers on social media will even sell such information for a fee, yet it is unclear whether their information is accurate or not.

Fansign culture is one of the main fan subcultures in the K-pop industry that blatantly encourages excessive consumer spending, and fan participation in these events shapes this dynamic. Through my experiences, I have observed and experienced firsthand how some vendors will encourage excessive consumer spending. These vendors also offered special perks for the top three to five fans who purchased the most albums, for example, autographed Polaroid photos.

But what do fans do with all of those albums? Many fans give the albums to friends or donate them to organizations. Some fans also try to sell the albums or just throw them away. The purchase of and disposal of these albums is part of neoliberal capitalist culture, but that practice highlights the environmental and sustainability issues caused by the unnecessary purchase of albums.

As for me, I gave most of my albums to friends, students, my favorite neighborhood stores, and even donated them to a charity that was willing to accept the albums. Disposing of all the albums was stressful. Later, I learned that some retail companies would not ship the purchases if the buyer requested them not to do so. So when I submitted my entries for fansigns, I asked the retail companies to mail me the autographed album and keep the rest. While this is one way to reduce environmental waste, there should be a better way to get into a fansign. The industry should find an alternative, for example, selling an entry for a set amount without having to purchase albums or merchandise.

Since the pandemic, there has been a dramatic increase in fan videos on social media that document fans' experiences of attending a virtual fansign. These allow us to explore other dimensions of neoliberal capitalist and consumer trends in K-pop fandom, particularly in regard to the unequal economic and social dynamics they foster. Many fan videos show the fan's careful preparations for the fansign. These videos include the fan's travel to the venue she reserved for the fansign, the preparations she made for the event, or even the food she ate prior to or after the event. Some fans will even reserve an AirBnB or hotel room to hold the event in a clean and trendy-looking room. They will decorate the room with balloons in the idol's name or flowers. The fan will wear nice clothes and jewelry and get a manicure. While fansign videos might not be as high quality or polished as *daepo* photographs—fan-taken photographs that will be discussed in the next chapter—Jungwon Kim notes that the edited contents are popular because these videos show fans' experiences of conversing with the idol, moments of the idol reacting to the fans' comments or requests, and also tidbits of unknown information on the idol which came up during their conversations.[6] But they can also throw into sharp relief the material and temporal costs of fan labor and its relationships to consumerist and gendered expectations of what true fan enthusiasm and loyalty must look like.

But most importantly, these videos focus on the idol's personal interactions with a fan. Through the one-on-one call interface, such videos can strengthen the viewer's parasocial relationship. While this kind of video emphasizes the idol's attributes, the fan in the video also becomes a focus of attention to viewers. The fan's unique conversation and relationship with the idol is one of the main attractions of fansign videos. Many fans prepare questions or missions for the idol to complete in a short time. Their interesting conversation or relationship can become the object of awe or envy to many other fans. For some fans who continue to attend fansigns several times, their testimonies can become a means to certify oneself as a loyal fan and even achieve some renown within the fandom. Hun-Yul Lee and Hye Min Ji argue that fan creators' individualized content can help these fans gain a kind of hierarchy or power in the fandom due to the popularity of the content they create.[7]

For their part, K-pop idols are advised not to give attention to, become close with, or single out a few selected fans. Many K-pop fans, while desiring to be recognized, want all fans to be treated fairly and do not want a few selected fans to receive attention or special treatment. When idols and their fandoms create a unique bond and friendship, it has to be a collective friendship, not an individual one. That said, many fans upload posts of photos or videos where a K-pop idol recognizes her due to her multiple attendances of previous fan events, or when an idol reposts a fan's artwork on his social media, or when an idol dons a gift that was collectively presented by the fandom. When fans were free to give gifts to idols, there were numerous posts on social media certifying that the idol wore what the fan gifted him. I myself have posted several photos and videos of my favorite idols remembering me due to my prior participation in fan events and witnessed other fans expressing envy or wistfulness that they might experience the same one day. Since the advent of social media platforms, this kind of culture of certifying what one wants to brag or show off to receive attention and envy is widespread and certainly not limited to K-pop fandom. But behind this act of certifying is the fans' collective desire—the desire to be recognized, to be seen, and to know that this idol-fan relationship is real, even if this must be seen through the experiences of others. To certify oneself, the fan has to perform much affective labor, and sometimes part of this affective labor is ameliorating the feelings of fans who were or are not able to participate in fansigns.

The neoliberal capitalist practices of fansigns shape the field of affective labor that is being performed in these events and through their mediation—labor that is performed by fans and idols. The necessity of purchasing many albums fuels fans' consumerist attitudes in believing that they are buying the idol's time and attention. Much of the idol's affective labor is fulfilling fans' requests at fansigns, mainly through *aegyo* and role-playing. These two acts sometimes overlap. In Korean culture, aegyo, a term that denotes a certain kind of cutesy or flirtatious behavior, is usually performed to appease the receiver, especially when the performer needs help or requests something. Performing aegyo has political connotations that reveal the gender dynamics and power structures between the performer and the receiver. Aegyo is considered a feminine trait in Korea and even a strength or virtue at times, and the performer of aegyo is usually in the weaker position.

Aljosa Puzar and Yewon Hong define aegyo as "a layered articulation of behaviours, gestures, vocal and linguistic adjustments, narratives and fashions that serve to enact child-like charm and infantilised cuteness" in South Korean culture.[8]

> Aegyo often appears in highly sexualised forms . . . and can often be related to distinctly adult hyper-feminine behaviours (while maintaining the aspect of winsomeness). . . . Performers of aegyo may and do often perform these infantilised cute behaviours as a form of private and intimate seduction or, more directly, when seeking favours or material rewards. . . . Many young women in South Korea adopt aegyo as a way to negotiate the imbalance of power within patriarchal, androcentric and ageist/gerontocratic environments.[9]

Through interviews, questionnaires, and field observations, Puzar and Hong contend that performances of aegyo reveal the unequal distribution of power in South Korean culture, as well as the importance that gendered performances play in negotiating or perpetuating such unequal distributions.[10]

Aegyo is also a common trope in K-pop performances. Stephen Epstein and James Turnbull analyze the visibility of aegyo in K-pop girl groups. In their study of approximately 100 music videos made by girl groups from 2007 to 2011, they learned that the singers express their desire for a male subject through "the repertoire of *aegyo*, a calculated performance of cuteness that infantilizes those (most frequently female) who engage in it in the hope of gaining the favor of a superior or attracting romantic attention."[11] It is therefore not uncommon to see many female idols having to perform aegyo on TV programs at a moment's notice. I found it very strange and even somewhat aggressive and oppressive that a male show host would suddenly demand that a young female idol "Do some aegyo [for your fans]" or "Show us some aegyo." Such demands for aegyo assume that aegyo is something that all Korean (female) idols should be able to do naturally, and that the (female) idol will willingly perform when requested. This expectation has expanded to male idols. *Weekly Idol*, a popular TV program, was well-known for requesting idols to perform aegyo for the television audience. In several episodes, many male idols cringe when the two emcees show examples of how aegyo is done well, and squirm with embarrassment when they perform it themselves.

As performing aegyo has become the norm in Korean TV programs as a form of "fan service," it is now even more difficult for idols to decline performing aegyo at fansigns. To many fans, the idol's lack of aegyo will indicate a lethargic, listless, and even ungrateful behavior, something that merits being "educated" and even cyberbullied. Thus, requesting idols to perform aegyo reveals how they can be subject to dollification, infantilization, and sexualization, not only by the industry but also by their own fans. I question whether idols should be coerced into performing, as demands for these kinds of performances from idols normalize both the culture of overconsumption that leads fans to feel that they are owed such labor and broader systems of gendered inequality that are interwoven with systems of unequal economic power.

Performing aegyo at fansigns usually includes doing or wearing something cute, like headbands with animal ears or ornaments. Asking the idol to wear something cute and/or enact cuteness reveals fans' desire to see (and document, photograph, or record) the idol's childlike façade. This kind of infantilization can become political because reducing an adult to a child is demeaning; and the politicization can be intensified when such performances are shared widely as videos. This reveals the complex power dynamics at play in K-pop fansign culture and its associated video presence. Because fans usually spend a large amount of money to be selected at fansigns, they tend to believe that they have bought the idols' compliance with their requests to perform aegyo and role-playing, and through videos, this logic can be extended outward to include other fans. Yet as some fans can and do find this entertaining and even empowering, it cannot be said to be equalizing if we consider the hierarchical gendered dynamics at play.

While aegyo is something one might perform quickly on their own, role-playing is a more arduous kind of affective labor. In a role-play, a fan pretends to be the idol's girlfriend, wife, or mother, etc., and stages a fictional scenario. Role-playing is an extension of the parasocial relationships constructed by fans. In K-pop, digital media and technology intensify the feeling of being copresent with the idol, creating an illusion of intimacy and proximity. This facilitates parasocial relationships and attachments to an idol, which can help fans become attached to the idol, and encourage their participation in fandom activities. When forming parasocial relationships, fans might posit themselves as the idol's "girlfriend fan," "wife fan," or even "mom fan." Depending on the type of fan they are, many fans make specific role-playing requests at fansigns, such as asking the idol to pretend to be his or her romantic partner or spouse during the fansign. While some fans delight in this kind of role-playing with idols during fansigns, others express distaste at pressuring idols to perform in a way that might embarrass them. Notably, such feelings may be exacerbated when they create tension with an idol's sexuality or other aspects of their identity.

The problematic issue of performing aegyo and role-playing is the unequal power dynamics inherent in these acts, as well as the limiting gendered and sometimes sexuality-related norms that can be reified through them. Even if the idol does not want to perform them, he/she might find it difficult to decline the fan's request. An idol might even feel pressured to do whatever the fan wants. Many fans might believe that they have bought the right to demand that the idol do what they want during the fansign time. In addition, because the industry often fosters these parasocial relationships, some fans also believe that recreating those relationships is an idol's rightful duty. Sooah Kim reminds us that such affective labor on the idol's part becomes an important criterion in evaluating their performance, even as important as their dance or vocal abilities.[12] Viewers may feel vicarious happiness and a sense of accomplishment after viewing the fan successfully completing her conversation with the idol, especially if she was able to make the idol answer important questions or complete cutesy tasks. In this case, it is the fan who becomes as important as the idol in making the video interesting—and also in shaping K-pop's relational dynamics. Moreover, these kinds of videos motivate other fans to make similar videos and upload them on social media. They will each try to showcase how their conversation with the idol was especially cute—which can also overlap with it showing particular power over the idol.

At Jiwon's fansigns, I have seen him appear briefly embarrassed when a fan asked him to do something cute. But he always did what the fans wanted. Many online memes show female idols acceding to ridiculous requests from male fans; their facial expressions show moments of embarrassment or exasperation, despite their best efforts to be professional and perform the affective labor requested of them by fans. Because of the gender and power dynamics in Korean culture and society, declining to perform aegyo is more difficult for female idols when male fans make requests, even when these requests are experienced as inappropriate or demeaning. Among the thirty fans I interviewed, nearly all confided that while they enjoy watching fansign videos of idols performing aegyo, they prefer fansigns in which fans do not pressure idols to perform aegyo too much:

A (FEMALE, 20S): I prefer fansign videos in which the fan is having a pleasant conversation with my bias. At first, I liked watching videos in which the fan gives the idol cutesy and fun missions, but as video call fansigns continued throughout the pandemic, most of the fan missions were repetitive and similar to each other and I could see that the idol felt pressured to do them.

B (FEMALE, 20S): There is a fan who did several video calls with Haechan, and I like her fansign videos because her questions or missions are clever and refreshingly witty. And because Haechan conversed with her several times, he looked comfortable in the fansign videos and spoke in a way that I could see he was at ease. I like fans who make idols feel comfortable. Rather than making idols complete missions that they do not like, I want to see fans cheer and encourage them.

C (FEMALE, 20S): Some fans will request missions that kind of cross the line. It feels uncomfortable watching the idol become uncomfortable.

While opinions varied, it is notable in these interviews that the kind of aegyo that is valued is of the creative or non-repetitive variety, while forms that make the idol visually uncomfortable are considered "too much." *Affective labor* as a term was not used in these descriptions, but fan responses honed in on the ways that coerced affective labor can materialize visibly uncomfortable emotional and bodily impacts.

Based on my research, I contend that the capitalist structuring of fansigns does not just exist alongside but gives form to a field of power marked by asymmetries, albeit temporary, of power between fans and idols. This flows both ways—fans may have to spend excessive amounts of money to engage; idols may have to service fans through gendered performances of powerlessness. In this dynamic, the labor that is performed may be building bonds, but the resulting community being formed may be a markedly hierarchical one. Here, even if gender roles are being temporarily "switched" between fans and idols, fan labor can contribute to the maintenance of (and in some cases, even eroticization of) underlying financial and gender disparities. Writ large, such disparities negatively impact fans individually and as a group, making the material and relational dynamics of K-pop the subject of continual discussion among, rather than only about, fans. This may in turn be influencing alternative creative fan video practices that are more narrowly focused on performances of creative and individual fan DIY labor.

"Album *Kkang*" and "*Tapkku*" for Fun: Fan-Made Videos of Opening K-Pop Albums and Decorating K-Pop Photo Card Sleeves

"Hot sauce *gipi* dip that," sings Mabokpil, her hands fluttering excitedly above three copies of NCT DREAM's *Hot Sauce* album. In her right hand is a small orange box-cutter knife, shaped like a carrot. Mabokpil is a popular YouTuber who uploaded her first video in March 2021.[13] While her YouTube channel is comprised of videos that show various K-pop activities such as listening to and singing K-pop songs, unboxing albums and merchandise, and creating scrapbooks, the videos rarely reveal Mabokpil's face or personal information and merely show her hands handling the K-pop albums or merchandise. Despite such anonymity, numerous K-pop fans find her unique aesthetics, humor, and singing skills compelling, and her YouTube channel has garnered attention and popularity among K-pop fans in a short time, attracting more than 200,000 subscribers.

"Everyone, I am finally doing the album *kkang*," Mabokpil announces, her fingers hovering above the albums. Like fansign videos, these K-pop "album kkang" videos, also known as "unboxing" videos, have become highly popular since the COVID-19 pandemic along with fansign videos. Compared to other kinds of vlogs that require more extensive preparation, these album kkang videos only require K-pop albums or merchandise to unbox, and the simple setting of such videos has encouraged numerous K-pop fans to film and upload their own album kkang experiences. While some fans reveal their faces and use their real names, many fans choose to film only their hands and albums and use nicknames or pseudonyms like Mabokpil.

These videos share the spontaneous moments and candid reactions of fans opening new K-pop albums for the first time. Such performances imbue what might otherwise be an outmoded media artifact in the age of digital streaming, the physical album, with excitement and allure. "Ah, I am so nervous," Mabokpil groans as she picks up an album. "Even my voice is shaking." In such videos, the fan shows off her purchases and findings from the unboxing. At the same time, these videos present a vicarious moment for other fans who cannot or will not purchase the album. The main attraction of these videos is seeing both the fan's reaction to the album and also the album content itself. Similar to other genres of reaction videos, the fan's candid response showing honest exclamations or unexpected outbursts is the highlight for many viewers. This kind of affective labor not only stimulates fans' desire for consumption, but also satisfies the viewer's curiosity vicariously through the visual practices of performing deokhu.

Such performances by the video deokhu plays an important role as/in affective labor. By observing or experiencing indirectly, these videos can create a feeling of shared experience and even connection between Mabokpil and the viewer. These vicarious experiences can motivate the viewer to mimic Mabokpil's reactions or create similar videos of unboxing CDs or merchandise. As such, vicariousness operates in important connective ways in fan culture.

"Renjun, please," Mabokpil pleads while rubbing NCT DREAM member Renjun's photo card against the album. "You don't *have* to come out, but it would be nice if you could!" Mabokpil lets out a happy squeal as she unwraps the album. "Is this the poster?" she asks as she holds up a folded piece of paper. "Let's start with the poster!" she exclaims as she unfolds the poster revealing NCT DREAM member Mark's face. "Mark! Your pants look so comfortable," she remarks. "Where is it?" Mabokpil asks as her hands flip through the album looking for the photo cards. The viewer sees her left hand finding a photo card which is placed face down in the album. "Ok, let's go. One, two, three!" Mabokpil counts and quickly flips the photo card. "Jeno!" She shouts and slams the desk with her fist in happiness. "I love Jeno! He is so handsome," she marvels as she holds the photo card to the camera for a better view. She prepares to flip the second photo card. "One, two, three!" When the photo card reveals her favorite member, Renjun, Mabokpil gasps and slams the desk with both fists. Her candid emotional reactions during the unboxing are one of the main features that the channel's subscribers find interesting. "Hurray!" Mabokpil whistles in happiness. "Shall we look at the album?" she asks as she flips through the album page by page. "Oh, don't hide that handsome face," she chides a member with long bangs. Mabokpil comments on each photo, exclaiming over the NCT DREAM members' style. Some are compliments on the members' handsome features and some are complaints to the members' stylists or album designers. "Why do they make it like this?" she admonishes, pointing to certain parts of the album with her finger.

As seen in Mabokpil's video, many fans perform a popular ritual in which the fan will rub the unopened album with a lucky charm or fan-made talisman, hoping that the album will contain her favorite member's photo card. Most K-pop albums do not contain all of the band members' photo cards and will only contain one or two photo cards that were previously randomly inserted. Thus, finding a photo card of one's favorite member is not guaranteed with the purchase of the album(s). Thus, when the fan opens the album to find her favorite member's photo card, the viewers can also feel a sense of happiness and satisfaction.

Within the past decade, photo cards have become an important aspect of K-pop fan activities. Fans showcase their photo card collection on their social media accounts and use photo cards to mark their fan activities. One popular practice is bringing your photo cards to concerts, fan events, and also quotidian venues such as restaurants and taking photos with the photo card. By doing so, fans certify themselves as enthusiastic and loyal fans who are always with their bias in sentiment. Fans will trade and buy/sell photo cards with other fans via social media accounts, with pricing for photo cards ranging from a few dollars to a few thousand dollars. The rarity of a given photo card can become a main factor in determining its value.

Similar to the fansign videos, many of these videos will show the lead-up to the unboxing—the fan purchasing the albums at the store or receiving a delivery, setting the containers up in a room, and showing her anticipation before the opening. Many fans will open more than one album, which is usually followed by the sharing of observations on the album. These videos also motivate other fans to create similar videos on social media. In these kinds of videos, the fan's personality—for example, their humorous commentary or interesting critiques—and content—their narration of personal stories about or observations of the albums and music—are the most important factors that determine the video's popularity.

Eunkyo Kang states that the most basic rules that make up the album kkang are probability and luck, which makes the practice akin to the pleasure of gambling.[14] Such fan rituals of rubbing the unopened album with a lucky charm or fan-made talisman are created to offset the inevitable frustration that gambling brings. And because the entire process of unboxing is shared online, it forms a consumption circuit that constantly stimulates fans' desire to purchase. Unboxing is both consumption (due to fans' purchasing) and labor (in that it generates profits by encouraging other people to make purchases). Therefore, album kkang becomes a representative form of K-pop affective labor in the era of platform capitalism, where the lines between play and consumption, and play and labor, are blurry. Moreover, it is also important to consider possibilities where this is by no means a closed circuit—not everyone who watches album kkang is necessarily going to buy the featured product. The forms of vicarious engagement, and often even pleasure, that this genre of video deokhu labor can elicit can also be thought of as its own entity that exceeds the consumption circuit.

Along with fansign videos and unboxing videos, another popular trend that emerged during the COVID-19 pandemic was *tapkku* ("decorating the photo card sleeve," called "toploader") and *seukeuraep* ("decorating scrapbooks") videos. K-pop fans create banners, calendars, dolls, key holders, photo books, planners, postcards, and many other products that celebrate K-pop and its idols. These are often exchanged among fans, through venues such as concerts or meetups, or via digital and postal networks. The literature on fandom has described the exchange of products among fans as a gift economy. The exchange of these products among fans is not profit-driven, but sustains the cohesion of the fandom community through giving and receiving handmade products, as well as the circulation of videos documenting or responding to such exchanges. Jungwon Kim examines how K-pop fans engage in not only video-making but also producing and consuming fan merchandise in addition to the consumption of K-pop official goods produced and sold under K-pop labels.[15] This is important, Kim argues, because such practice reveals how a fan "appropriates, transforms, and replaces" the dominant culture of mass-production in K-pop.[16]

During the pandemic, fans documented their own process of decorating photo card sleeves and scrapbooks, showcasing their creativity and artistic talent. Using beads, glue, stickers, and tweezers, fans take meticulous care to make photo card sleeves according to their tastes. This can be understood as part of a broader DIY culture that aims to customize, personalize, and differentiate one's possessions apart from the mass-produced merchandise and to show one's performance of care at the same time. As they decorate the sleeves, they talk about the idols or their personal issues, enabling the viewer to create parasocial relationships with the fan. Viewers can witness the fan decorating the photo card holder or sleeve or scrapbook and feel a sense of accomplishment, or even inspiration to craft something similar. These videos also motivate fans who make similar craftwork in response to film and upload their own videos on social media. After decorating their own sleeves, fans will take photos of them with their deokmates, showing off not only their artistic talent, but also their own fan community. These fans will take photos of decorated sleeves holding their biases' photo cards at concert venues, fan events, or restaurants.

As seen from the case studies above, the level of consumerism in K-pop fandom today far exceeds that of other generations of K-pop fandom. There are a variety of factors that explain such consumerism—fans' heightened parasocial relationships with idols and other fans due to technological innovations, the industry's never-ending promotion of newly created merchandise, and even peer pressure in the fandom. Fans look up to other fans who perform an astronomical level of consumption and fan videos created by these fans promote bulk-buying and spending. However, as the tapkku video trend indicates, there has also emerged a parallel DIY culture that celebrates creative processes that, even when they revolve around a piece of mass-produced official merchandise, are about showcasing more slow-moving artistic labor to create a one-of-a-kind item. Similarly, the broader trend of gift-making and exchange also subverts neoliberal capitalist logics of consumption. When such creative labor is performed and circulated via fan-uploaded videos, it is the performing deokhu and the fan community that they cohere, rather than any specific group or idol, and this is what becomes a central focus of attention in K-pop's fan video circuits.

Conclusion

In this chapter, I have explored emerging modes of K-pop fan videos and examined how these videos become a space in which fans perform their fan identity and showcase their unique ideas and styles while shaping norms of relationality and exchange. Central to this process is an ongoing negotiation of the unequal power dynamics that undergird and even challenge deokhu values of inter-relationality and comradery between fans and idols and among fans. In fansign and other genres of videos, the performing deokhu can gain space to build a connection with an idol and other fans; at the same time, the extent to which this connection is predicated on excessive mass consumption of merchandise and inflected by gendered scripts of both fandom labor and idol aegyo influences its affective possibilities. Motivated by the circulation of fansign videos, there is a growing discussion among fans about how fan events do or should structure behaviors and relationships in K-pop.

Similarly, fan videos of unboxing and photo card sleeve decoration help shape K-pop fan practices and their relationship to both forms of horizontal community-building and consumer culture inequalities. By viewing other fans perform fan identity through affective labor, one can feel a sense of vicarious accomplishment and motivation to create similar experiences or even videos. At the same time, many of these videos encourage excessive spending and wastefulness in fan practices. Recently, K-pop fan organizations such as Kpop4planet have voiced their opinions about creating sustainable practices in K-pop, such as encouraging fans to stop bulk-buying albums and collect less merchandise.[17] While numerous fans acknowledge environmental concerns in K-pop fan practices, it is not easy for fans to abandon their activities unless the industry and management companies devise strategies to create fan events that are sustainable as well. As K-pop's global rise continues, many fans feel it is imperative that the industry and fans find a collective way to reduce wastefulness and exploitation in K-pop fan practices, which may help contextualize the prominence of strategies of DIY decoration and mutual gift exchanges seen in tapkku videos. Indeed, beyond the activities of the video deokhu spotlighted in this chapter, there is a broader upsurge of fan-created events and texts through which fans materialize in online and physical spaces their own perspectives on K-pop's meanings and possibilities. The next chapter turns to fan practices that further alter or push against the neoliberal capitalist industry's structures and create an archive that curates and narrates fan experiences and affective states.

3 • The Archiving *Deokhu*

Curatorial and Narrative Practices in Fan Photography and Writings

In September 2022, a social media post warned Koreans not to go to the Hongdae area of Seoul on September 13. "That day [September 13] is the birthday of Yeonjun, Sungchan, and Hyunjae. Cancel all appointments in the Hongdae area immediately." The social media post referred to the many K-pop *saengka*—a portmanteau of *saengil* (birthday) and *café* meaning a fan-produced event that K-pop fans organize to celebrate their favorite idol's birthday—that frequently take place in coffee shops of the Hongdae area. After the post went viral, similar posts emerged every month, alerting people of the upcoming saengka. These posts highlight how fan-produced events focused on celebrating idols and their music in personal terms reminiscent of the ways family and friends might have become a popular subculture in and beyond Korea. These events are important not only for the immediate communities they form, but because of the ways fans document and share documentation of such happenings. Beyond occurring informally in the moment, such practices of documentation and sharing also produce an archive of fan-driven activities, which may then itself serve as a platform for future fan-produced experiences and events.

Fan events like saengka are not typically sponsored by management companies or orchestrated primarily for profit. Instead, they represent an alternative space where fans perform types of affective and organizational labor that strengthen social cohesion among fans by bringing them together—sometimes literally—in spaces in the physical world, and other times through documentation of fandom experiences that constitute what might be called a *deokhu* archive. Made up of myriad individual and collective enterprises, the deokhu archive, as I conceptualize it here, centers content produced by fans documenting elements of K-pop and its communities from fan perspectives.

This chapter focuses on fan practices that originate and circulate beyond the commercial infrastructures of K-pop orchestrated by management companies and other commercial stakeholders with a particular emphasis on how fans archive these aspects of K-pop music, community, and fandom through documentary formats of photography and writing. Specifically, it examines two types of fan-made products—photography exhibitions and published writings—which together illustrate how fan labor documenting K-pop centers fan-specific vantage points and values in the culture of K-pop. While sharing many linkages with the digital and video deokhu activities described in the previous chapters, these activities are notable for the ways they bridge digital and physical, as well as commercial and personal, spaces. They also intervene in fandom's material and temporal dimensions, as deokhu archiving practices materialize what might otherwise be ephemeral experiences into textual and visual objects that can be shared in multiple formats across time and space, thereby expanding possibilities for community building, creating continuity in the culture, and even offering spaces for critical reflection.

Despite a renewed academic interest in K-pop fandom activities, very few scholars have examined fan-produced exhibitions and memoirs archiving fan-produced events as an important subculture of K-pop fan labor. But these are important to study for several reasons. While K-pop fandom is often highly mediated by commercial digital platforms, it also takes place in and through individual fans' production and consumption of archival materials documenting aspects of fandom that fans express as important to themselves communally and personally. Photography exhibitions and memoirs are places where fans, adopting positions of authorship and curation, articulate themselves as cocreators of K-pop's meanings. Meanings they center in these kinds of documents include K-pop as a site of genuine love and bonding (especially among fans); K-pop fandom as driven by agential fans with capacities for critique and self-reflection; and K-pop as a site of personal development and transformation, and also perhaps as a lever of social change. Therefore, these are essential realms and practices through which fans give meaning to and strengthen relationships with K-pop and with one another.

To analyze the archiving deokhu and the significance of their (often her) affective labor, this chapter first examines archival practices in K-pop fan-produced photography exhibitions documenting fan-organized events. As the saengka example illustrates, fans produce pop-up exhibitions to celebrate events such as their favorite idol's birthday or a special anniversary—for example, the day of the idol's debut. Examining K-pop fans' activities in preparing, staging, and sharing the photography exhibitions elucidates the documentary labor they perform, which adds an important layer to industry-produced content that tends to center idols and music as products. Comparing fans' photographic and curatorial styles to those of management agencies reveals overarching patterns: fans' photos tend to center candid and even voyeuristic characteristics, and their curatorial style often caters to fans' desires, especially for intimacy and feelings of connection. To elaborate on this dynamic, I examine my own experiences viewing fan-produced exhibitions by first-generation K-pop idol Eun Jiwon's fan communities: two exhibitions from 2018, three from 2019, and one from March 2020. In addition, I examine the reception of these activities by viewing discussions about them that have appeared in online fan communities and social media.

Next, this chapter examines three memoirs written by fans of BTS—*Bangtansonyeondan anpadeon gwageoui na jonna bulssanghada* (How fucking unfortunate I was when I didn't stan BTS) by Deobeulyuar, *Oneurui halil: bangtan* (To do list: BTS) by Team Nunaz, and *Bumping into BTS* by Ji Kim, Mick Shin, and Jane Do. These independent publications give fans' autobiographical stories of constructing their identities as BTS fans and how *deokjil* (fanning) transformed their lives. On the other hand, Heera Oh's *Naneun naui paeni doellaeyo: gwamorip deokhureul wihan taldeok annaeseo* (I want to be a fan of myself: Exit guide for deeply immersed fans) shows the self-reflexive practices of a K-pop fan through a critical look back at her experiences. This chapter examines the ways in which the fans' memoirs materialize a public fan archive centered on fans rather than idols, documenting their transformative journey as K-pop fans, and furthermore, both revealing and complicating the stereotype of K-pop fans as brainwashed young girls; in reality, K-pop fans vary in age, ethnicity, nationality, and gender, and they actively construct meaning from their participation in fan activities, which they sometimes reflect upon in-depth in other artistic outlets, such as memoirs.

By examining these activities, I reveal how such exhibitions and independent publications centered on documenting fan-organized events, even as they can serve as a means of advertising and promotion for idols, can also exceed and provide alternatives to the neoliberal capitalist K-pop industry's main aims and practices. One way that the archiving deokhu discussed in this chapter intervenes in the production of K-pop fan culture is by documenting and contributing to activities in which fans exchange information with each other to corroborate an idol's authenticity. This is important because it influences the terms of K-pop's parasocial relationships between fans and idols, centering the fan value of authenticity in K-pop's promotional culture and making fans the arbiter of this quality. This has had an impact on fandom practices, as the archiving deokhu's documentation makes these events sources of community discussion. Moreover, because of the social stigmatization of fans, camaraderie and friendship with others achieved through fandom practices documented by the archiving deokhu create a safe space for fans to navigate their identities—including in terms of gender, race, and sexuality, but also as fans—in ways that promote reflection and debate on topics not centered by the industry.[1] The fandom practices examined in this chapter, K-pop fans' photography exhibitions and writings published by and about K-pop fans, become an alternative space for fans to document and reflect upon the communal and individual feelings, relationships, and sense of community that their affective labor of producing a deokhu archive creates.

Archiving All Your Moments in K-Pop Photography Exhibitions

During the "becoming-a-fan" stage of immersion in K-pop, many fans seek camaraderie and company with others in the fandom. Creating relationships with other fans can enable one to partake in fan activities and events more easily, due to encouragement from and information shared with one another. Furthermore, doing deokjil with another like-minded deokhu can profoundly shape this social experience. As Heejeh Ahn reminds us, it becomes meaningful because the deokhu can have her desires—which are often looked down upon or called delusions by non-fans—understood and approved by someone else in a safe space.[2] In other words, it is in these fan spaces that the deokhu subjectivity often crystallizes. Being part of a fandom can change or transform individual aspects of deokjil. And each fandom shares a collective memory of events, practices, and rituals that were constructed by fans.

Photographs play a pivotal role in the process. From the start, K-pop management companies have invested heavily in producing certain kinds of staged publicity photographs of idols for popular consumption. There also followed a journalism/tabloid industry. But fans themselves have also heavily invested in producing these images.

In K-pop fandom, a *daepo* is a fan who attends most in-person events of their favorite idol and regularly uploads photos or clips taken at such events onto social media. The Korean word *daepo* is translated into English as "cannon"; the DSLR cameras that many of these fans have been compared to cannons. Daepo photos are called *jikjjik*, short for *jikjeob jjigeun sajin*—informal photos taken by fans and not released from the idol's official accounts managed by the agency or media journalists. Significantly, most of these photos are taken from a fan-specific vantage point, and thus this labor produces an archive of K-pop fandom that centers fan positioning and subjectivity.

Daepo photography practices and modes of display span the physical and virtual worlds, as well as the personal and commercial ones. Most daepo will post "previews" on their social media accounts as soon as they have taken the photos. Later, they convert them into high-resolution photos to upload. Many of these will be close-ups that are airbrushed, edited, or photoshopped in ways that complement the idol or draw attention to specific elements of their appearance or performance. Such photos are not limited to the idol's stage performance, but also include candid moments, for example, the idol en route to the venue—in street clothes, perhaps casually sipping a Starbucks coffee—and then on his way home—waving to the fans from behind the heavily tinted car windows—or even checking in at the airport. Such photos can create the illusion of the fan seeing the idol in real time. In addition, the unposed photos can create a certain sense of intimacy that is absent from stage performances and their official mediation.

Over time, the K-pop fandom has developed an accepted code of conduct for the daepo. This differentiates the daepo from non-fan paparazzi. In general, the daepo will limit themselves to taking photos at or around the idol's officially scheduled appearances, as fans disapprove of photos being taken during the idol's unofficial schedule that is not announced by the management agency, deeming this behavior invasive. Fans who follow idols to unofficial schedules or personal excursions are viewed to be *sasaeng* fans or stalkers. Not all daepo are sasaeng, but there are suspicions of stalking that emerge when some daepo also take photos for idol schedules whose locations are unannounced. Fans will call someone out and organize against their photographs if stalking behavior is seen.

The daepo does not only take photographs, but also makes a range of decisions around editing and display. When the daepo selects which photos to upload to social media, they tend to choose photos that place the idol in the most flattering light. It is also common to feature close-ups of abs, arms, eyes, or hands, and to spotlight positions that portray an idol as cute, masculine, or sexy. Many of these photos will contain cues or inside references that only fans will recognize. These photos do not have to be as polished and airbrushed as management agency photos are—rather, photos that show the idol's idiosyncratic features and the fan's voyeuristic point-of-view can cater to fans' desire for intimacy.

On social media, daepo accounts are among the most popular fan accounts and have a large number of followers. Hun-Yul Lee and Hye Min Ji argue that fan creators' individualized content can help these fans gain a kind of hierarchical power in the fandom.[3] These accounts can become more or less popular depending on the quality of the photos and the frequency of updating. Because an idol's bodyguard or managers try to keep the daepo at a safe distance from the idol, and the daepo will sometimes be walking or running alongside the idol, clear photos and video clips from a steady camera are the ones that fans appreciate most. Some fans might prefer daepo photos to official photographs because they are less posed and seem more authentic. While there are copyright issues, especially when the daepo use their photos for commercial purposes, most management agencies will look the other way. Management agencies have come to realize that daepo photos, especially excellent ones, can help create avid fans and build the fandom. Most daepo insert their social media account ID or logo into their photos as a trademark and enforce rules about other fans using their photos for commercial purposes. For example, other fans may repost daepo photos on their personal social media pages, as long as they do not remove or tamper with the daepo's ID or logo. Some fans may also create unofficial merchandise with daepo photos, as long as they get permission from the daepo who took the photos first. Many daepo readily permit fans to use their photos on banners, bus and subway advertisements, and social media advertisements celebrating the idol's birthday. Popular daepo enjoy a special kind of authority, especially if the idol "likes" the daepo's photos on social media or uses them on his own social media profile. This kind of special recognition can create popularity but also jealousy and hostility among fans. Some daepo who have been cyberbullied have temporarily or permanently left the fandom or suspended their social media accounts.

Daepo sometimes stage pop-up exhibitions as well, in which the daepo prints and displays their images at venues such as coffee shops or galleries. For these, the daepo may select photos that they had been saving for such a special occasion. They might also take the opportunity to play with scale, as these venues allow for larger images than those typically viewed on personal devices. Attending fan-produced exhibitions helps elucidate their significance as an important K-pop fan subculture that contributes to the building of cohesive fan communities. In June 2018, I visited two exhibitions: *CODE:BLACK*, which was organized by JJIWONY WORLD, YOUNGiGi, GiHADA, EUNRO, and LISTENING SOUL, and held from June 9 to 10, 2018, at Gallery Orchard; and *Love, Inspiration*, which was organized by theloveGi and ONESPIRE, and held from June 6 to 13, 2018, at Tigre Blanco for the first seven days and at 57th Gallery on the last day. In June 2019, I visited three exhibitions: *G[ONE]:ZONE*, which was organized by CRUSH ON, theloveGi, EUNRO, and 68C, and held from June 1 to 2,

2019, at Gallery Onsu; *Logue*, which was organized by Reminiscence and Tamnikk, and held from June 1 to 2, 2019, at Gallery Won; and *ONE REASON*, which was organized by G MAJOR, and held from June 5 to 9, 2019, at Café Bom. The exhibitions in June 2018 and 2019 celebrated Eun Jiwon's birthday. In March 2020, I visited *2020 WONDER G1*, which was organized by EUNRO, and held from March 14 to 18, 2020, at Café Hoban, to celebrate the nineteenth anniversary of Jiwon's solo debut. Together, these events provided a window onto the dynamics and practices typical of daepo exhibitions.

Idols and management agencies have nothing to do with these exhibitions where daepo fans are the curators. The daepo photos are enlarged and mounted on the walls. Sometimes they are arranged in a collage or particular shape. To the public, they may seem no different from official concert photos or publicity photos. But for fans, each photo memorializes a special event, and it is important that they do so in a way that simultaneously documents the presence of the fan or the wider fandom community. For instance, for some viewers, a photo might tap into a fan's own specific memories of the details of the day pictured, allowing the viewer to be transported back in time and space to a cherished K-pop performance or encounter. In many instances, candid photos also capture aspects of an idol's characteristics that are especially talked about or valued among fans, such as particular facial expressions or hand gestures. When these contain information or themes that only fans may be aware of, and that they share and discuss with each other, they can reinforce feelings of bonding among fans. Some of these photos are offered for sale or gifted to fans. For example, when I attended *Logue*, my admission goody bag contained a scratch card and I won an enlarged photo of my choice from the exhibition. I won another enlarged photo after my social media review of *WONDER G1* was selected through a random drawing.

In addition to photos, some exhibitions also showcase replicas of discography, concert paraphernalia, and the idol's handwritten messages, as well as screenings of concert DVDs, TV stage performances, or fan videos. *CODE:BLACK* also included a garment that Jiwon had donned at his solo concert, and later threw into the crowd. Because this garment was custom-made, stitching together half of the fan club hoodie and half of the fan club T-shirt, it was not easily reproducible. The fan who had caught it at the concert had lent it to the exhibition. I saw many fans oohing and aahing to see the one-of-a-kind souvenir. The effort to include such material artifacts gives additional "liveness" and visceral connections to the 2D photos on display.

Figure 8. Eun Jiwon photography exhibition, *Logue*. Photo by Areum Jeong.

Figure 9. Eun Jiwon photos arranged in the shape of a heart at *Love, Inspiration*. Photo by Areum Jeong.

At these exhibitions, deokhu-produced merchandise such as banners, calendars, handheld fans, key holders, photo books, photo cards, planners, and postcards may also be offered for sale. Some creators will choose to keep the profits for themselves, and most fans do not object to this because they know how much time and effort are required to create exhibitions and merchandise. That said, the ethos of most fandom is to keep everything nonprofit and put the profits toward the idol, so these exhibitions often become opportunities for fundraising to support the idol in some way. For example, the orga-

Figure 10. Eun Jiwon's discography displayed at the *G[ONE]:ZONE* photography exhibition. Photo by Areum Jeong.

nizers of *CODE:BLACK* notified fans through Twitter/X that all profits from photobook sales would be donated to an animal shelter in Jiwon's name. The photobook would include not only photos exhibited at the event but also unreleased photos. Fans who ordered the photobook would also receive other small fan-made merchandise such as photo cards, postcards, and stickers. The organizers kept their promise: after the exhibition, they uploaded a donation certificate issued by Korea Animal Rights Advocates, a civic organization for animal rights in Korea. This was especially meaningful because Jiwon, who had had dogs all his life, was well-known among fans as an animal lover. This kind of detail could have also motivated fans to attend the exhibition and order the photobook, knowing that the profits would be spent on donating to charity in Jiwon's name. In a similar manner, the organizers of *Love, Inspiration* notified fans through Twitter/X that all profits from the exhibition and merchandise sales would be spent on purchasing birthday gifts for Jiwon. After the exhibition, they posted detailed explanations and photos of each gift they had prepared and delivered to the management company. And G MAJOR donated profits from *ONE REASON* to the streaming support team and album sales support team, indicating the importance fans place on streaming activities, as seen in chapter 1. The streaming and album sales support teams are made up of fans who encourage other fans to support their favorite idol's by streaming music and purchasing albums to boost rankings. In a way, these fans' invisible labor was being made more visible as labor through G MAJOR's gesture.

Wenfang Zhong argues that in the digital environment, *homma*—a portmanteau of "homepage" and "master," and another slang term for *daepo*—can hold three roles: users of social media, producers of idol-related content, and consumers of the idol industry.[4] Thus, they are the most active and passionate social media users, content producers, and also distributors of content. When examining the fans who are consumers, producers, or sellers in birthday cafés and photo exhibitions, Jungwon Kim argues that the fans involved in this economic activity share a kind of collective identity as members of the fandom.[5] Although each fan performs different roles, there is a communal goal they want to reach through participation in these activities. Through carrying out birthday cafés and photo exhibitions as a ritual and festival, fans mutually confirm the fandom as a collective identity, one whose significance cannot be captured solely in market terms. Derek Kompare views such fans as curators who bring their curatorial skills to the fandom.[6] These fan curators are significant because their curations shape and help build fan experiences.[7]

Many of these exhibitions take place in coffee shops. For example, *ONE REASON* took place at Café Bom, and *2020 WONDER G1* took place at Café Hobean in Seoul, Korea, where organizers created special cup sleeves to celebrate the occasion. Due to their popularity, many coffee shops and gallery spaces in Seoul invite fan exhibitions and accept applications to stage them via social media platforms. These coffee shops and gallery spaces will then use their social media to promote exhibitions that take place in their space, reaching audiences that may never have heard of an idol. Conversely, this can bring fans who would never have heard of the café or gallery to the business. Some venues charge rental fees, but some coffee shops do not, as providing the space to fans for an event can prove lucrative. Tamar Herman writes about how such café events can provide the fandom with a sense of happiness and a space in which to connect with one another.[8] Through these exhibitions, the organizers create spaces where fans can celebrate special occasions and feel a sense of community. Through viewing photos that document past events and significant moments, fans can make new friends and connections. After the exhibitions, many fans post photos on social media.

Figure 11. Cup sleeve event celebrating Eun Jiwon's birthday. Photo by Areum Jeong.

Figure 12. Photography exhibition within the birthday café. Photo by Areum Jeong.

These events help strengthen relationships and ties within the fandom, helping to create and document the ways K-pop's parasocial relationships are transmuted through such practices of photography and writing into horizontal community ties between fans, who agentially determine K-pop's meanings and possibilities.

Archiving Experiences of Fandom Through Independent Publishing

Just as daepo archiving labor communicates experiences between individual fans and the wider fandom and offer spaces to reflect on relations, some others do this with words rather than photographs. Fans themselves have engaged in publishing about their lives and experiences in the fandom, often turning to independent publishing to share their experiences and insights in material form.

Meanwhile, *dongnip chulpan* (independent publishing) in Korea has become popular with the growth of independent bookstores since the 2010s. Amateur writers can write and illustrate their own stories, design their book covers, and use design software to create layouts. They can then hire a vendor to publish a certain number of books, and offer the books for sale to independent bookstores (as well as via online marketplaces). Despite the time and effort, there has been an increase in independent publishing by K-pop fans. Independent publishing allows fans to create their publications without having the publishing industry regulate the content, distribution, or promotion. Notably, many of these publications center on fans' autobiographical stories of constructing their identities through fandom and how this transformed their lives. As such, these publications not only document specific fan activities and practices but also create space for reflection upon K-pop fandom in ways that attend to the subjectivities of fans. Notably, many of these accounts do not appear to be written to be sold to "outsiders"; rather, they address other presumed fans as the intended audience.

To write their memoirs, some deokhu will crowd-source funding from other fans and then use social media to keep contributors apprised of the date of publication of the work whose creation they supported. In this way, the writers can promote their works and also ensure sales. Fans will purchase these books to read about their idols *and* to learn more about the fan-author. Indeed, these are often inextricably linked in works produced in this genre. As Matt Hills reminds us, "becoming-a-fan" stories help scholars consider "how the process of first experiencing fandom, and initially embracing a fan identity, can be lived as self-narrative, and how it might be discursively framed."[9] Examining available memoirs offers insights into an archiving fan practice that, while potentially remunerative for an author, derives from outside practices initiated by management companies and other commercial actors who seek to profit from and through the expansion of K-pop fandom in its parallel focus on the author instead of only the idol. Here, we will consider works written by BTS fans, as members of this fandom to date have been especially active in self-publishing.

Deobeulyuar's *How Fucking Unfortunate I Was When I Didn't Stan BTS* is a memoir about becoming a BTS fan, and through this, transforming their life in meaningful ways. The author, who had lost motivation in school and their career, began to set goals and resolved to become a better person after engaging in fandom practices.

> Mornings that used to be painful became exciting and happy. I would start the day by being surprised at clips and photos I had not seen yet, excited at new schedules, and sharing my feelings with people like me. There could be unexpected accidents throughout the day, but whether you face those with a happy state or a weary condition, there is a big difference in the damage intensity and recuperation level. I would look forward to each day. I would await the next day and the next.[10]

These feelings of motivation, which sound like they may be mitigating previous feelings of stress and depression, grow as the author becomes more immersed in BTS's oeuvre—and specifically in the fan culture produced by fans online, which this memoir portrays not as obsessive or repetitive, but rather as invigorating. As they describe,

> After my first concert, I became determined to do my best as them [like they do]. After my second concert, I became determined to work hard and go to the next concert. There was a renewed motivation for my work. Not just to earn the money for tickets, but I wanted to live a life I myself am proud of, and proud of in front of them.[11]

These experiences are not singular to this author, having been described anecdotally in fandom discourse and even in academic research. According to Derek A. Laffan's study on positive psychosocial outcomes and fanship in K-pop fans, more intense K-pop "fanship" significantly predicted increased happiness, self-esteem, and social connectedness.[12] Possible reasons for K-pop fan affiliation with improved general psychosocial outcomes are that K-pop may confer a sense of belonging upon members of online K-pop fan community groups; K-pop may be considered as an alternative to mainstream Western pop culture, which has been critiqued for individualism, white normativity, and associated discrimination of people of color; and fan users of social media technologies may provide an increased sense of accessibility and connection to their idols.[13] Deobeulyuar's work underscores that this connection is mediated by and through connections with other fans doing affective labor in service to other fans.

Notably, all three independent memoirs examined in this chapter reveal how becoming BTS fans made the authors happier. Similarly, Team Nunaz, a group of four BTS fans in their thirties who wrote *To Do List: BTS*, discuss how their lives were transformed after becoming BTS fans:

MYONG: Passion! I realized that there is still passion in my life. I was motivated by Namjoon to listen to more music, read more, and see more art to cultivate my own taste. I became determined that I should not give up on my taste. . . . As you grow older, there are times when you have to give up on your taste, but I became determined that I wouldn't. I began to love myself as a person who has a particular taste.[14]

This personal transformation that the authors of both *How Fucking Unfortunate I Was When I Didn't Stan BTS* and *To Do List: BTS* describe receiving inspiration and motivation from BTS, and feeling a sense of belonging within the fan community. It is precisely such affect that becomes the basis not just for personal transformation but also for social change, a process into which these memoirs also provide important insights.

In *To Do List: BTS*, the writers' conversations are transcribed thematically, leaving intact, for instance, the jargon and slang used in fan communities and the varying pronouns used to describe BTS. These choices about written language may facilitate readers' empathy and identification with the authors, especially if they too are BTS fans. Like Deobeulyuar's *How Fucking Unfortunate I Was When I Didn't Stan BTS*, the members of Team Nunaz discuss how they became ARMY, what they find most interesting about BTS and their fandom, and how becoming ARMY has changed their lives. In doing so, they provide critical documentation of fandom practices and experiences they deemed to be collectively and personally valuable:

SIRI: Although they are stars, I feel like a trust relationship is constructed and they even seem like my friends sometimes. I feel like I am listening to their deepest innermost thoughts when I need them the most. They post on Twitter immediately after finishing an event and livestream when they want to talk more deeply, so they feel like close friends.[15]

BOMI: Fans have always wanted to know behind-the-scenes stories and what my favorite star is thinking, so I think it is impressive that they fulfilled that need. Previously, fans' knowledge was limited to what you only see on TV. But they voluntarily post behind-the-scenes clips, ask how we are more frequently than our own families, and post their deep thoughts on the official café. I think these kinds of contents are what distinguished BTS.[16]

Such exchanges support Michelle Cho's analysis of how BTS's uses of social media to provide "real-life contents"—for example, "behind-the-scenes clips of their backstage antics, dance practice videos, member vlogs, and gif-length video selfies"—help fans become emotionally attached to the group.[17] Rebecca Chiyoko King-O'Riain states that this "digital intimacy" and emotional investment are the main factors for K-pop's global popularity.[18] In addition, Team Nunaz advertised their publication plans via social media and crowd-sourced funds via Tumblbug. Because they could not release the book until the costs of publication were fully funded, the support of the fan community was important. This also shows that many fans were curious about what BTS fans had to say about their idols.

Bumping into BTS, by Ji Kim, Mick Shin, and Jane Do, was published in 2020 in both English and Korean. Each author wrote one chapter about how they became a BTS fan and how it has affected their life. In addition, the text draws upon the work of cultural theorists and news articles to give a critical and reflective perspective on ARMY, BTS's fandom, and the K-pop industry.

Kim, who "enjoys writing about cases that cannot be explained by a dualistic view of consumers and producers," teaches Korean popular culture in the United Kingdom and describes herself as an "acafan of popular culture," using scholar Henry Jenkins's term for an academic who is also a fan. As an acafan, she clarifies that this essay is a record of her "personal history and feelings," based on her "growing zeal and passion for BTS over the past few years," which is of "great importance" in her life.[19] For Kim, this book is a personal account of her journey as ARMY and an alternative archive for the fandom. Coauthor Shin discusses the many activist activities ARMY has organized and how the fans' interaction brought "a sense of belonging stemming from the premise that we all love BTS, so likely share similar (or relatable) tastes, values, and political views." Shin continues: "What I witnessed in this fandom was an equal, horizontal, and mutually complementary relationship between BTS and ARMY."[20] Do, a producer in the entertainment industry, states that "the real purpose of this essay is to argue that, in the K-pop industry, where BTS, among many other boy bands and girl groups' merit are connected directly with their commercial value and profitability, we need more open discussion on the support and protection of the young would-be K-idol trainees."[21] Her observations of idols and fandoms in the K-pop industry, combined with her newfound interest in and affection for BTS, have made her more attentive to issues related to mental health and sustainability, especially among young idols and trainees.

How Fucking Unfortunate I Was When I Didn't Stan BTS, *To Do List: BTS*, and *Bumping into BTS* are stories of and by fans. When reading these stories, fans can identify with the authors. They may also feel a sense of community and empathy with the authors, as indicated by reviews and informal fandom discussions of the works. While the memoirs are personal, they encourage fans to interact with each other offline or online; and indeed, all these narratives discuss specific examples of how doing so enriched the authors' own lives. In addition, these activities go against the current trend of consuming content via social media in an extremely short time as these activities require time and waiting. Indeed, a major theme present in all these works is the authors' illustration of sustained engagement with thinking about K-pop and its communal and personal significance as a form of entertainment, a form of community, and even a labor system. This is an essential quality of fandom that their work materializes and archives, and also expands the possibilities for, as new personal and academic collections of works offering increasingly in-depth analyses based on personal experiences.[22]

This emphasis on giving sustained attention to K-pop and its impacts in published memoirs can in some cases provide critical insights into fandom that discusses or advocates for interventions in dominant practices of performing deokhu. Heera Oh identifies herself as a K-pop fan for more than twenty years, and she still is a fan of several K-pop acts. In her book, *I Want to Be a Fan of Myself: Exit Guide for Deeply Immersed Fans*, she narrates how she fell in love with several K-pop musicians, the different fan activities she engaged in, and how she exited each fandom. After publishing *I Want to Be a Fan of Myself* in 2020, Oh published *Exit Guide for Deeply Immersed Fans*, a revised version of the book, via *Brunch*, an online writing platform in 2021.[23] In an interview, Oh explained the reason for doing so: "For those who want to exit the fandom or want to engage in fan activities while maintaining their life but find it difficult, I decided to upload the revised version on a space that anyone can easily access."[24]

While studying creative writing during college, Oh dreamed of publishing her writings. She was also crazy about the K-pop group Seventeen—so crazy that she could not focus on her daily tasks. Although her love for Seventeen did not waver, she did not like that her affection for the group affected her life in unproductive ways. To exit from the fandom, she decided that she would have to separate her identity as a member of Carat (Seventeen's fan club) and objectively reflect on herself. She decided to write about how to exit the fandom to motivate herself. She also thought that there might be someone else having the same dilemma and decided to publish her writings for those fans. At first, she was nervous about uploading her writings on exiting the fandom on social media platforms, where commentary could quickly become overwhelming, so she decided to publish more conservatively via print. In addition, she chose independent publishing instead of submitting her manuscript to a mainstream press, because she wanted to do everything by herself. It took her approximately three months to finish the manuscript, one month to produce it, two weeks to print it, and three weeks to contact independent bookstores and place the books in their stores. In total, she printed 300 books for approximately 1 million won (less than $1,000). The books sold out and many independent bookstores asked her to reprint the book, but she decided to revise it and upload the revised version on an online platform that is easily accessible to readers. She wanted to make it free for viewing, which reflects the ethos of the fandom she valued and archived through her work. After the book was published, she was surprised to receive messages from many readers. These readers were fans who shared the same thoughts as Oh and could identify with her as a K-pop fan.

In the first book, Oh writes:

> This book is not a diary of praising fan activities, but more of a diary trying to exit the fandom. Even at this moment, I am trying to get away from them [biases] physically and mentally. Because fan activities are a part of, no, more than half of my life, it is so difficult to exit the fandom. Therefore, I started writing to motivate myself. In caution that I might return to the fandom, this book is an oath that I will exit from it.[25]

However, her position becomes slightly different in the revised book as she writes,

> I can't say that I am not engaged in fan activities anymore because I am someone's fan. However, the way I do things now is different from

> that of last year. Although the methods might be similar, the perception, attitude, and immersion toward fandom are completely different. So I decided to revise the book. The previous book strongly recommended exiting the fandom. The revised book can be said to encourage healthy fan activities and exiting fandom in a healthy way.[26]

Oh writes about her experiences when she was deeply immersed in her bias(es) and cautions readers that one should do deokjil in a healthy manner without losing oneself. Based on her experiences, Oh divides fanning into seven levels: muggle level, knowing level, interest level, *ganjaep* level, light level, core level, and master level.[27] Referring to the Harry Potter series, the "muggle" level signifies the state in which one does not know about idols and does not have any interest in fanning them. The knowing level is when one is aware of idols and some of their works, but does not show any clear interest. The interest level is when one becomes interested in an idol's works and voluntarily watches his shows, but does not show further interest in learning about his characteristics or personality. The ganjaep level refers to the Korean term *gan bogi*, which means testing the waters or poking around with some interest. Oh describes the ganjaep level as semi-fanning because one becomes more active than the interest level by actively searching for information on the idol or subscribing to his social media accounts. To describe the light level, Oh prepared a series of questions for the readers:

> Are you a member of the official fan club?
> Did you create a fan account on Twitter or Instagram?
> Do you subscribe to paid-membership fan platforms (for example Weverse, Universe, Lysn, etc.)?
> Do you have something about your bias in your room?
> Did you attend a fan meeting or concert?
> Did you purchase an album, DVD, or any official merchandise?
> Did you purchase something that is not your preference, but your bias's preference?
> Is your YouTube viewing queue related to your bias?
> Is your Melon app's intimacy degree higher than 96?

If one answers yes to more than three of the questions above, Oh states that one has become a light level fan. The core level fans would say yes to all of the questions above. In addition, Oh states that having two or more *deokmates*—close friends who keep each other updated on the idol's activities and go to events together—can accelerate one from the light level to the core level in a short time. The master level fans are those who devote their time and money entirely to fan activities around their favorite idols.

Oh describes herself as having been a core level fan and writes that fans' daily lives are as busy as those of idols.[28] When she would get up in the morning, she would check the fan club webpage and social media platforms for newly updated information. She would watch the idol's contents on YouTube while eating breakfast. On days off, she would meet with other deokmates and attends fan events together. Oh looks back at how much her fanning was rooted in her daily life. After a series of *taldeok*—exiting the fandom—Oh looks back at herself and questions the problems she encountered when she became deeply immersed in K-pop idols.[29] First, she writes that she tended to escape from reality due to unhappy situations. Second, she writes about the problems of immersing too much into and identifying with idols. Third, she stresses the importance of being a fan of oneself and investing in oneself as one would do with an idol. In the final chapter, Oh encourages fans to love themselves more than they would love a K-pop idol.[30] She provides advice for new hobbies and ways to better oneself. Oh's book, through documenting her own experiences, shows the ways in which fans can be self-reflexive and deokjil in a healthier manner. More concretely, it eschews simplistic binaries of fanning as completely good or bad and identifies aspects of fandom practices—for instance, devotion to ideals, working hard to achieve goals, showing support—that can be productively mapped on to healthy practices of self-development and community engagement.

Some archiving deokhu reflect on K-pop and its fandom practices via fiction, potentially using their own experiences to portray the deokhu experience in ways that will resonate with fans. Challenging the stereotype of the childish K-pop fan, Heejoo Lee's novel, *Phantom Pain*, which was published by Munhakdongne and received the Munhakdongne College Fiction Prize, follows M and Manok, avid fans of a K-pop idol named Mingyu. Lee portrays the protagonists' affect throughout the novel, first from M's perspective, then from Manok's, and then from that of a boy (also named Mingyu) who is in love with Manok. This work, a novel that builds on the author's experiences and contains memoir-like aspects, can also be seen as a contribution to the deokhu archive, one that documents and reflects upon fan-specific vantage points and values. In her interview with Lee, novelist Sol-a Yim comments that this is the first Korean novel to portray K-pop fans and their experiences and emotions in such depth.[31]

Phantom Pain describes the ways in which fans construct their own identities and subjectivities through their activities and relationships with other fans. In doing so, the text illuminates fans' agency and genuineness, defying the stereotypes and gatekeeping in mainstream Korean literature. The book opens with M befriending Manok at fan activities:

> Whenever I spoke, Manok added something, and whenever Manok added something, I chimed in, and in this manner, there was no possibility of the conversation ever waning. I was overjoyed when I saw her, as one tends to be with a new friend. During check-in for a TV music program, I saw Manok approaching from a distance and found myself as thrilled to see her as I would have been to see a member.[32]

In this description, the author archives the intimate affective register fans are able to inhabit together while also documenting sites of idol performances as central staging grounds for cementing and deepening friendships among fans. These themes continue in the portrayals of the rituals of fandom, which emphasize member interactions and even analogize them to shared religious devotion:

> When the members were active, new information gushed forth on a daily basis, and the conversations between me and Manok stretched on without end. Like travelers that had set out on a holy pilgrimage together, we recited endless catechisms. New stages, new broadcasts, new events—we were always there with the members. We voraciously devoured the information pouring out.[33]

As these examples illustrate, when fans build parasocial relationships with their idols, they get to know the idols through their online personas and through their relationships with other fans. Through in-person or digital contact, fans analyze something that their favorite idol posted or did. They keep each other up to date and recommend and share fan resources. Fans who become close friends even travel to sites that have some association with their favorite idol.[34] In this context the Korean term *seongji sunrye*, meaning "pilgrimage," refers to fans visiting the same restaurants or tourist destinations that the idols had, and placing themselves in the scenes that had appeared in their idols' music videos or variety shows. In these ways, fans build camaraderie with each other. Similarly, M and Manok keep each other company while standing in line for TV show tapings and share information that only fans would care about, such as what Mingyu had had for lunch. By participating in fan activities together and exchanging information, fans strengthen their parasocial relationships with idols by corroborating authenticity. M and Manok typify K-pop fans, showing how, as King-O'Riain argues, "'liveness' is central to the process through which fans feel emotionally close to their K-pop idols and facilitates fans' investment 'in real life' emotional interactions with other fans."[35] While strong relationships among fans can help make their idol more successful, these ties also expand into activities beyond supporting the idol, such as activism and social change. Although there might be a risk of generalization in the novel, its sensitive portrayal of M and Manok's most mundane activities, and its interpretations of them as meaningful sites of social connection, is realistic.

Moreover, *Phantom Pain* also archives the social stigmatization of fans, and how their camaraderie and friendship with others create a safe space to navigate their identities not only as fans, but as people. The narrator muses,

> Before I met Manok, I would utter these precious feelings to other people when it felt like there was no way to contain the love that was overflowing in my heart. The majority of them listened silently, but I could sense their indifference and quiet mockery. Blunt people did not bother to conceal that they found me pathetic. Polite people smiled and made great efforts so that their magnanimity would be noticed. More than contempt, it was this tolerance that exhausted me. But having fallen in love, I was capable of uttering only one thing, and was gradually reduced to a person of few words.[36]

Expanding upon how society belittles or dismisses K-pop fans and fans' reactions to such dismissiveness, the narrator notes,

> The love affairs of others are always a laughing matter, but ours in particular becomes an easy target for criticism. Simply because our love is for people in a specific occupation. Our words and behavior are treated as if they were age-inappropriate, or some kind of sickness. I know what they say about us. "Crazy bitch, she's lost her mind . . ." Because they consider us a flock of young girls, because they don't think we pose a direct threat, they're even more like this. But people who love are strong. Whenever someone sneers at our love, I silently pray to myself. In the way that only those who know devotion and passion can so desperately pray, I know my prayers are the most effective. Whenever people cast scornful glances at us or swear as they pass by us in front of the broadcast station, I always think: "You'll never know what it's like to love this much."[37]

Although K-pop has evolved from a local subculture into a global phenomenon, there is still prevalent criticism of fans who are either viewed as "a flock of young girls" or as "age-inappropriate" adults. Yet, despite the stigma, fans maintain the special sense of community and sincerity that binds them to their idols, and to each other as well as to emotional states that they cherish, such as devotion and love. The efforts on the part of both the fans and idols make that sense real. Fans connect with idols through various fan activities and form parasocial relationships which are viewers' imaginary relationships with media figures. Although this closeness between fans and idols can appear to be only an illusion, it is this sense of intimacy that fosters a connection between fans and idols and encourages participation in fandom activities. Like other works written and published by fans, *Phantom Pain* memorably archives the generative, reflexive, and even reparative work of performing deokhu in its emotional and social complexities.

Conclusion

While there are plenty of popular portrayals stigmatizing fans as slavishly controlled by the industry that their labor supports, this chapter has examined activities through which the archiving deokhu documents and organizes fan experiences, creatively sharing their works and thereby providing spaces for communal and individual reflection on K-pop and fandom. By focusing on two types of fan-made products—photography exhibitions and published writings created by fans—it explores how fans produce and preserve an archive that functions not only to promote K-pop idols but also to document and shape K-pop's significance for fans themselves as individuals and members of a community. While enmeshed in certain respects in the neoliberal capitalist structure of the K-pop industry, fans' attempts to curate and narrate experiences of fandom also exist beyond this structure and create alternative creative spaces within it. This can be seen in the kinds of publishing ventures fans have undertaken, such as independently publishing memoirs and first-person analyses, as well as in photographic exhibitions whose creators depict K-pop from the perspective of fans themselves.

When fans create, document, and share their own curatorial and narrative portrayals of K-pop fandom through photography and writing, they center what their participation in fandom brings to them, from emotional feelings, to insights into their own experiences, to materials for self-transformation and the making of communal bonds with other fans who participate in the affective worlds they cocreate. While the industry operates through the constant production and proliferation of instantly consumable new content, the archiving deokhu takes a different approach, emphasizing alternative positionalities, temporalities, and orientations to fandom.[38]

4 • The Exiting *Deokhu*

Acts of Disengagement, Resistance, and Collective Mobilization

On November 12, 2018, former fans of Kang Sung Hoon—a former member of the first-generation K-pop boy group SECHSKIES—filed a lawsuit against Kang and his fan club manager for fraud, particularly for embezzlement of fan donations. This lawsuit was the first of its kind in Korea, in which a K-pop artist was sued by his own fans. Fans also accused Kang of fraud for his abrupt cancellation of a fan meeting that was scheduled to take place in Taiwan in September 2018, and in regard to tax evasion around several fan club events. In response to Kang's recent misdemeanors, fans self-organized a legal team to take matters into their own hands. They actively investigated Kang and his fan club manager, posted updates via online discussion boards, called attention to their suit via social media, and shared their actions with media and news outlets.

This chapter examines what happens when fans choose to stop performing the traditional *deokhu* role of supporting and promoting the K-pop industry. The deokhu "exit" from fandom, as I call it, can include a range of behaviors, from high-profile acts of collective mobilization against misbehaving idols, to forms of resistive activism performed within the fandom, to more gradual forms of disengagement such as fans distancing themselves from their idols. It can also involve the mobilization of affective labor that fans have performed in their deokhu roles toward new goals, some of which may seek to reform or transform aspects of idol behavior, the industry, or fandom rather than entirely leave K-pop behind. The deokhu exit, therefore, should be understood as a multifaceted phenomenon enacted differently by distinct individuals and fan communities. And furthermore, I argue, conceptualizing the deokhu exit in terms of labor does important work in revealing another instance of fans performing the *materialization of affective labor* that powers K-pop's endurance and transformations.

To examine the deokhu exit and the labor it entails, first, this chapter focuses on the former fans' lawsuit against Kang, reconstructing how fans effectively organized a legal case against the artist's corrupt and deceitful actions. Through a close examination of fans' discussions via online communities, interviews, news articles, and social media, I demonstrate how collective fan activities mobilized to enact change in the industry or impose accountability on performers can heighten fans' sense of agency. Moreover, examples of successful deokhu activism that heightens feelings of fan agency in the industry can trigger broader interest among fans in orchestrating or participating in future collective actions. Such collective actions may focus on reforming or impressing accountability on individuals in the industry; but they may also take aim at structures in which the industry operates and which it helps to shape, such as broader patterns of sexual harassment and female exploitation.

Extending this point, this chapter secondly examines fans' responses after Lucas—a former member of K-pop groups NCT and WayV—was accused of engaging in inappropriate relationships with young women. Here, K-pop fans mobilized to express their desires and expectations for idol behavior, particularly related to their intimate relationships. While some fans responded to Lucas's actions by turning away from K-pop, others found empowerment in the movement to hold idols accountable to community standards of conduct, and by participating in debates this action provoked around gender relations in K-pop.

And third, this chapter examines Seyeon Oh's documentary film *Seongdeok* (*Fanatic*) (2021), which depicts the director's and other fans' experiences of exiting fandoms due to idols' misdemeanors. Through their labor of creating and exhibiting this film, Oh and other participants created opportunities for representation, dialogue, and even community formation around what might otherwise be a solitary and disconnected action. Significantly, the film's depiction of the deokhu exit ultimately advocates for reflexive practices in fanning, which include attention to performances of care and a vision for systemic changes in the larger entertainment industry.

Scholars have examined how fans can express dislike or hate through individual or communal activities. For example, via "active and resistant readings" and "rejecting producer actions that run contrary to one's own conception of the narrative," fans can "rework and rewrite it, repairing and dismissing unsatisfying aspects, developing interests not sufficiently explored."[1] How fans do this has changed in step with technological and other norms. In the pre-internet era, fans might have written letters and made phone calls to express their dissatisfaction. Then, as C. Lee Harrington and Denise D. Bielby found in their research during the mid-nineties, fans began to use more public forums like the daytime press and electronic bulletin boards to make complaints known.[2] New media such as digital and social media provide key platforms for fans to express criticism. This kind of communal hate or dislike can "produce just as much activity, identification, and meaning, and 'effects' or serve just as powerfully to unite and sustain a community or subculture" as admiration or love.[3] More recently, Euro-American fan studies have explored how fan activism, such as letter-writing campaigns and boycotts, have influenced media cancellations, casting calls, and even public political issues through charity fundraisers and protests.[4] However, explorations of how fandom and activism forged around causes of complaint directly related to actors in the industry come together and complicate each other are particularly underrepresented in K-pop studies. My research shows how the heightened sense of collective agency that emerges from fandom practices, such as all those discussed in earlier chapters, can shape and be shaped by fandom labor directed toward activism that critiques, resists, or demands changes in aspects of K-pop that violate fan expectations and values.

Together, the three case studies featured in this chapter provide insight into how K-pop fandom is a highly organized, networked community with specific communal goals carried out by affective labor which is never solely coopted by the industry into supporting its preferred structure and products. Focusing on incidences in which this affective labor is organized toward acts of resistance or enforcing accountability, as well as the operative processes in which fans exit fandoms while also mobilizing action, reveal how fans seek to materialize their own desires and expectations in K-pop, including codes of conduct that are expected from idols. Especially through mobilizing online to have their voices heard, fans organize and direct their collective affective labor toward undertakings that impact not only the industry and its performers, but also fans. Notably, they often focus their efforts on economic or sexualized abuses of power that harm fans.

After *Deokjil*: *Wandeok* and *Taldeok*

There are distinct terms for describing different processes of exiting K-pop fandom. *Wandeok* is a portmanteau of the Korean words *wanseong* (completed) and *deokjil* (fanning), meaning completed fanning, which could be used as either a noun or verb. This signifies a situation in which a fan disengages from the fandom after her love for the idol has been completed. This also implies that the fan did not leave the fandom out of hate or spite, but rather perhaps grew out of it or chose to move on to other things. It implies that although she might not keep up with the idol's news or engage in fan activities anymore, the fan might still care for the idol or at least hold positive sentiments about the idol or her time spent performing deokhu.

On the other hand, *taldeok* implies a more abrupt or sudden act of exiting the fandom. Combining the words *taltoe* (exit) and *deokjil*, it signifies a situation when a fan disengages from the fandom due to a specific reason. In my interviews with several fans who experienced taldeok, the reasons for leaving a specific fandom can be grouped into three categories. First, the fan leaves because she finds a different idol to love. Second, the fan leaves voluntarily because she loses interest in the idol or finds the idol undesirable or negative due to a particular issue. For the second category, the reasons can include behavioral issues ranging from the idol being sloppy in appearance to disapproval over an idol's dating life or how an idol is rumored to conduct intimate relationships. And lastly, the fan leaves somewhat reluctantly or unexpectedly because the idol's misdemeanors have suddenly come to light—that is, there is a scandal of some kind that creates a widespread reckoning around the idol.

In general, the Korean media and public expect celebrities to uphold ethical standards and behave in a "moral" way. Often, prescriptions for morality are quite conservative, reflecting expectations of heteronormativity, patriotism, deference to elders, abstinence from sex and drugs, etc. As mentioned above, fans also maintain certain standards for idols' behavior that can overlap but also be distinct from the general public's expectations.

As the industry constantly hints that fans' labor of love is crucial for idols' successes, many fans believe that their affective labor and financial spending are the key to idols' fame; in turn, they believe that idols' behavior should meet their standards. Even if unstated as such, there can be transactional logics at play, and there is sometimes a particular focus on idols owing fans certain comportment around dating and relationships. For example, some fans believe that an idol should not date or get married; otherwise, he is going against an established code of conduct that requires idols to remain single and thus at least theoretically "available" to fans. Therefore, when an idol is reported to be dating or engaged, some fans leave the fandom. This can extend to other aspects of what might in other contexts be considered "personal" behavior. Stephanie Choi reminds us how fans' expectations of an idol can affect the fandom:

> It is difficult to maintain a solid fan base when idols are caught dating, drinking, smoking, or doing any other type of "misdemeanor" outside

> the dorm. Fans do allow their idols to go outside but urge them to take responsibility for what they do. Because fans are the ones who are paying the "debt"—by buying concert tickets and merchandise—idols must show gratitude and appreciation by "working hard," not by dating in public or going out to bars and clubs.[5]

As we saw in previous chapters, fans expect transparency from idols along many dimensions, as evidenced for instance by frequent communication with fans via their social media accounts or official fan club websites. Values of authenticity and intimacy in communications go hand-in-hand with expectations for idols not to deceive their fans. What counts as deceiving can be broadly construed. However, based on many previous accounts in which fans became angry or upset, acts of deceiving fans might include taking fans for granted, for instance by not showing gratitude that fans expected to see, or flouting fans' expectations by having a romantic relationship revealed. These acts are described as fan *giman*. The term means a cheat or lie and can also be used as a verb, as in to "cheat" or "lie to" someone. Because K-pop fandom is largely built on the affects of parasocial relationships, feeling betrayed or jealous can greatly influence fans' attitudes about an idol and even about performing deokhu more generally.

Due to Korean society's collective moralism, Korean fans' expectations toward idols can sometimes differ from those of non-Korean fans.[6] For example, some say Korean fans are more conservative or strict about some issues, such as expecting prohibitions on romantic relationships; in contrast, non-Korean fans tend to be happy for their favorite idols who are in romantic relationships. In these circumstances, it is not uncommon to see fans argue with each other on social media. Mathieu Berbiguier and Younghan Cho remind us that Korean fans, while acknowledging non-Korean fans as important players in their fan activities, can also view non-Korean fans in a hostile manner when they do not conform on certain issues, and contrasting ideas about idols' romantic relationships are a prominent area of discord.[7] In sum, fans from different places may have different expectations of idol behavior, and thus they may cite different reasons for exiting the fandom when their exit is related to an idol's actions.

In the aftermath of wandeok and taldeok, many fans struggle with how to deal with their emotions, memories, and material remnants, mainly albums and merchandise. Fans who wandeok-ed frequently choose to keep their albums and merchandise because those objects hold sentimental value even though their love for the idol may have waned. Conversely, many fans who have taldeok-ed choose to dispose of their albums and merchandise because they hold negative sentiments toward the idols they had once loved. Many fans choose to sell their merchandise on online secondhand marketplaces or via social media. In addition, many fans delete their fan accounts on social media or photos from their mobile phone and computers. Fan accounts with large numbers of followers will also signal their disengagement by putting "CLOSED" on their profile, indicating their exit from the fandom, and posting an explanation of their disengagement. These explanations provide a rich archive of deokhu exits. Many of these statements disclose in a detailed manner the reasons why the fan left the fandom; on the other hand, some decide to write ambiguous and brief statements. The statements that receive much attention from other K-pop fans are the ones that reveal the fan's authentic experiences and sincere thoughts that other fans empathize with.

For example, one *taldeokmun* (taldeok statement), which received much attention and empathy, writes about the deokhu's experience exiting the fandom after losing herself in the process of her full immersion in fandom (https://m.blog.naver.com/oha08/221623326849). In her statement, the fan details how she became a superfan of the idol, and in that process, sacrificed her career and well-being by prioritizing the idol rather than her own self. The fan explained that she was leaving the fandom not because her love for the idol waned, but because she decided that her activities were not healthy and she wanted to become a better person. This statement received much sympathy not only from fellow fan club members but also from fans of other groups as well, showing that many K-pop fans share similar experiences in putting the idol ahead of themselves. On the other hand, many other taldeok statements hold idols accountable for their sloppiness in appearances, fan service, or stage performances. Reactions from other fans to these statements shows that there is consensus among fans about their expectations for idols to behave in certain ways.

Regarding the third category of taldeok, K-pop has seen no shortage of idols' crimes and misdemeanors. Previously, fans have displayed acts of agency in calling out both K-pop companies and idols for insincere or otherwise negative acts—they demanded that companies stop mistreating idols and asked idols to rectify problematic behaviors and better themselves. Such moments can be traced back as early as the second generation of K-pop fandom. Eunkyo Kang views the second generation of K-pop fandom as the defining time in which fans "became citizens," meaning they take matters into their own hands, acting on their own will, in support of their biases, or in support of values they believe idols or companies should better uphold.[8] For example, in March 2008, fans of SUPER JUNIOR bought shares of SM Entertainment stock to voice their opinions about SUPER JUNIOR's future plans.[9] This is also when one sees the early beginnings of the "support culture" that is prevalent in K-pop fandom today, as we saw in chapter 1's discussion of JYJ. Seung-Ah Lee discusses how JYJ fans "organized both on- and off-line to protect the artists they love and defend their rights as consumers, for example, laboring to place JYJ's album to the second spot of the year's list of best-selling albums. They have also initiated a remarkable array of self-policed activities, ranging from publicity campaigns to consumer boycotts, against SM."[10] For example, 9,817 JYJ fans raised more than 150,000,000 won in eleven days for 120 bus advertisements. In 2019, fans of BLACKPINK protested and demanded that YG Entertainment make concrete plans regarding the four members' future solo activities.[11] These are a few of the many cases in which fans acted out in favor of protecting or supporting their favorite idols, with the main adversary often being the management companies that are perceived to have wronged idols. Thus, it is important to see that this support culture now intersects and sometimes gives way to more aggressive forms of collective organizing. It is not unusual to see several hashtag *chonggong* (mobilized/organized attack) by different K-pop fandoms on social media today. Such a description implies a greater sense of agency among fans, and a keener awareness of their own capacities to inflict cultural sanctions or economic damage.

But there are cases in which even the most avid fans will turn away and exit the fandom or even become vicious antis and haters of idols or management agencies. With the resurgence of feminism and the #MeToo movement against sexual harassment and assault in Korea, fans have called out idols who displayed insincere behavior regarding gender equality and/or made controversial comments regarding gender and sexuality. For instance, some fans called out RM of BTS for the misogynist content in his lyrics from "Joke" and "War of Hormone."[12] In response, Big Hit (BTS's management, which is now HYBE), responded promptly that they have "become aware that BTS's lyrics contain misogyny and contempt, regardless of the creative intent, and that women may feel uncomfortable."[13] In addition, they promised to be more reflective and "continue to refer to the points raised and issues in future creative activities."

There have been more widely controversial and even criminal cases in which idols have been accused of and punished for sexual offenses and misogynist acts. In 2019, the Burning Sun scandal included K-pop idols such as BIG BANG's Seungri, Jung Joon-young, FTISLAND's Choi Jonghoon, CNBlue's Lee Jong Hyun, and Highlight's Yong Junhyung. These prominent idols were involved in sexual assault, prostitution, drug distribution, creating hidden camera footage of sex with women, tax evasion, and police corruption.[14] In

November 2018, it was revealed that the police of Seoul's Gangnam district tried to cover up a fight at a nightclub that was owned by Seungri. An investigation revealed that the club was a site of "drug dealing, prostitution and sexual assault fueled by date-rape drugs, according to police."[15] Furthermore, several male celebrities and their friends had exchanged text messages that included discussions of drugging women and sharing sexually explicit videos which were filmed and distributed without consent. CedarBough T. Saeji reminds us that this criminal scandal reveals broader patterns of gender disparity, violence against women, and institutionalized patriarchy in South Korea, which are also not unrelated to the misogynist representations of women in K-pop, and the actions of some of its stars.[16] In this case, fans responded not only by exiting their fandom, but also calling out the stars involved and demanding justice for those they harmed.

While the Burning Sun scandal remains the most extensive and high-profile scandal, it has not been the last. By turning now to the specific examples of (1) former fans of Kang Sung Hoon filing a legal complaint against him (the first case in Korea in which an artist was sued by his own fandom) and (2) Seyeon Oh's film *Seongdeok* (*Fanatic* [2021]; an independent documentary film that traces the director's journey of fanning and disassociating with the now-fallen K-pop star Jung Joon-young, who was also involved in the Burning Sun scandal), we can see how fans perform affective labor in effectively organizing action against idols' corrupt and deceitful actions. These examples show fans to be active consumers who are not shy to voice their opinions and mobilize for actions ranging from calls for justice to a collective deokhu exodus.[17]

Former Fans Versus Kang Sung Hoon

Controversy over the actions of SECHSKIES lead singer Kang Sung Hoon started during his solo career following the group's disbanding in 2000. Kang was accused of not repaying a loan of 1 billion won he had borrowed from three acquaintances in 2011, and he was arrested on March 30, 2012. Kang was found guilty and received a year and a half imprisonment and two years' probation. In 2013, four additional complaints were filed. Kang was sued four times for fraud from February to July 2013, and the total amount claimed by the complainants amounted to 2.7 billion won. However, the prosecutors dismissed the charges at the end of the year. In April 2015, Kang was sued for fraud again, but the prosecutors dismissed the charges in August. Due to his previous misdeeds, Kang joined the list of artists who were banned from appearing on MBC, one of Korea's biggest broadcasting stations. This certainly kept Kang from making an effective comeback, and his media appearances during this time were minimal. But in April 2016, *Infinite Challenge*, a popular TV program that initiated SECHSKIES's reunion, was able to get Kang back on air.

After the successful reunion via *Infinite Challenge*, five members of SECHSKIES signed a two-year contract with YG Entertainment, one of Korea's biggest entertainment agencies. Since 2016, the group released four albums that included both new and old tracks, performed in several cities in Korea and Japan, and appeared on various Korean TV programs. The group even placed first on TV music programs in 2017 for their new single "Be Well," and received several awards from Korean music award programs from 2016 to 2018. It was not common for first-generation K-pop groups to regain popularity after a long hiatus, and SECHSKIES became a successful model for first-generation K-pop groups that wanted to attempt a reunion. Both old and new fans engaged in fan activities to support the group after a sixteen-year hiatus, and even received the BOF (Busan One Asia Festival) Best Fandom Award in 2017 for their collective efforts. Jeff Benjamin's analysis of the group's newly gained popularity proclaimed that the "'90s/'00s generation of K-pop fans are supporting their favorites while these acts gain new fans in today's YouTube age."[18]

During these times, Kang strived to rebuild his career. As soon as the group reunited, Kang released a call for members for his personal fan club, Hoony World, in July 2016. After holding several fan events for approximately a year, Kang recruited new fan club members from December 21, 2017 to January 21, 2018. In 2018, Kang seemed more determined to expand his profile and rebuild his career. In addition to fan events and solo concerts in Korea, Kang pursued fan meetings overseas in Taiwan and Japan.

On August 31, 2018, Kang's Taiwan fan meeting, which was scheduled for September 8 and 9, was canceled abruptly. The Taiwanese media reported that Hoony World canceled the event one-sidedly, which resulted in the Taiwanese agency that was in charge of organizing the event losing 100 million won.[19] As a response, Kang posted on his fan club website that the Taiwanese agency deceived him in the process and the Taiwan government did not issue him a visa. Kang wrote that he had tried to proceed with the fan meeting even if he was not going to profit from it. The Taiwanese agency responded that such claims were false, as they had already deposited Kang's fee, and sued Kang for fraud.

As the argument between Kang and the Taiwanese agency escalated, fans' positions regarding Kang and the incident shifted. At first, the majority believed that the Taiwanese agency had swindled Kang. But as the Taiwanese agency consistently provided evidence that refuted Kang's statements—for example, contracts and documents prepared for the event, recordings of an employee's conversations with Kang and Kang's fan club manager, and screenshots of email exchanges and text messages with Kang and Kang's fan club manager—suspicions about Kang's actions intensified. Through such evidence, fans were able to see that the Taiwanese agency was cooperative in planning and preparing the fan meeting until the sudden cancellation of the event. Except for claiming that he was innocent and duped by the Taiwanese agency, Kang remained silent. He did not provide evidence supporting his claims, nor was he proactive about issuing refunds for fans. Many fans were disappointed at Kang's silence, which further escalated their suspicions that he had been in the wrong. In addition, fans were also enraged to view the fan club manager's sloppy, unprofessional work (via the documents that the Taiwanese agency provided) and her disparaging claims made toward fans, as she was caught referring to fan events as "cash cows."

This was not the first time controversy arose regarding certain fan events organized by Kang's fan club. During the previous year, fans had experienced several unprofessional handlings of fan events and duly complained about such issues via the fan club website. Fans asked Kang either to hand the reins of the fan club to YG Entertainment (which manages SECHSKIES as a group) or hire a new professional fan club manager. But Kang refused; he was adamant in his response, posting that he would not proceed with either option, but would make an effort to improve conditions in the future. Despite his promises, fans' complaints regarding several events were not resolved—and remain unresolved up to this day.

In light of the Taiwan fan meeting incident, fans' suspicions regarding other issues emerged.[20] When the Taiwanese media reported that Kang's fan club manager is actually his girlfriend and also one of the key figures in the handling of the Taiwan fan meeting, fans were outraged, because the fan club manager was also responsible for the unprofessional handling of several fan events during the past two years. Fans reported that the ways that past fan events were managed seemed corrupt and illegal. For example, in April 2017, Hoony World organized a screening celebrating the twentieth anniversary of SECHSKIES's debut and asked fans to donate to charity. Many fans participated in the donation, and a total of 100 million won was raised at this event. But Hoony World never notified fans of when and to whom they donated the funds, as is typically done after such events. When fans requested that the fan club release public documents providing the whereabouts of the funds, Hoony World posted a belated statement saying that preparations for the event were much more expensive than their estimated budget and thus they did not have any funds left over to donate to charity. When fans demanded to view the contracts, receipts, and bank account statements in association with the event, Hoony World posted an estimate sheet written before the event, not the actual receipts or bank account statements. Because figures in the estimate sheet are subject to change, the estimate sheet cannot be seen as a legitimate document that supports Hoony World's claims. Moreover, fans noticed that some figures in the estimate sheet were unusual. For example, the screening venue rental fee was stated as 60 million won. Acting themselves as amateur investigators, fans contacted CGV, the Korean multiplex cinema chain that provided a venue for the screening, and confirmed that the venue rental fee is 6 million won, which is one-tenth of what Hoony World provided on the estimate sheet. Some expenses, including the venue rental fee, seemed to have been inflated several times more than the original price. These suspicious circumstances led to accusations of embezzlement of fans' intended charitable donations.

In addition, the Taiwanese agency provided additional information that added new charges to Kang's misdeeds. The Taiwanese agency claimed that Kang's fan club manager signed a separate contract, aside from the official contract, when signing the fan meeting contract.[21] This separate contract states that a certain sum of money is delivered to a certain individual in addition to the fee stated in the official contract. In general, a separate contract is used for tax evasion purposes. While it seems that Kang's fan club manager was fully aware of tax issues, some argue that there was a possibility that Kang himself may not have been aware of these issues because he did not sign the contract and the fan club manager signed on his behalf. But the Taiwanese agency claimed that there was no way Kang could not have known, because his fan club manager was also in a relationship with him. The Taiwanese agency filed both civil and criminal suits against Kang and his fan club manager. Again, it is notable that these machinations became public knowledge due to the demands initiated by fans.

Furthermore, Kang was also accused of illegally using YG Entertainment's name in preparing for the fan meeting.[22] When the Taiwanese government requested the Taiwanese agency's materials regarding Kang's affiliated agency in order to issue a visa, Kang's fan club manager sent an email to the Taiwanese agency in YG Entertainment's name, stating that they received all materials regarding the Taiwan fan meeting and asking the Taiwanese agency to cooperate with Kang. When they were questioned later by news reporters, YG Entertainment claimed that they were not aware of any of this. Together, all of Kang's and his manager's protestations about the Taiwanese company's errors and their own innocence came to seem unbelievable and suspicious to many fans and even journalists covering the unfolding scandal.

During the whirlwind of accusations and news reports, fans' discussions were very active online, especially via the DCinside fan community, which serves as a hub community for most K-pop fandoms. Fans tirelessly posted new information about Kang's misdemeanors, expressed anger and disappointment, and also discussed what to do that would be in SECHSKIES's best interests. The majority of fans seemed to want to continue to support SECHSKIES and other members except for Kang. As a result, numerous fans demanded that Kang be excluded from the group's concerts that were scheduled to take place on October 13 and 14, 2018.[23] Fans declared that they would boycott the concert if Kang performed. Fans expressed their opinions to YG Entertainment via email, fax, social media, and the SECHSKIES official fan club website. Kang posted an apology via his fan club website, but fans were not appeased. Days had passed and Kang did not provide any evidence refuting the Taiwanese agency's claims, nor did he come forward with an explanation about allegations about his fan club manager/girlfriend. In the same manner, Hoony World did not provide sufficient information regarding the whereabouts of the charity event donations. Fans decided to take the matter into their own hands.

On September 20, 2018, fans posted a request via the DCinside fan community board demanding that Kang clarify his and his fan club manager's "unethical and illegal acts."[24] On September 21, 2018, fans posted a collective statement demanding that Kang leave SECHSKIES permanently. Such requests and statements were initiated and carried out through a collaborative process. Fans expressed their opinions via email, fax, social media, and the SECHSKIES official fan club website. Shortly after the release of the fans' statement, YG Entertainment announced that Kang would be excluded from the October concert, but did not comment on other demands or issues.

On November 12, 2018, approximately seventy fans, all of whom had donated funds at the 2017 screening event, filed a complaint with the Seoul Central Prosecutors' Office on charges fraud and embezzlement.[25] It was the first case in Korea in which an artist was sued by his own fandom. The fans who had previously donated funds for the screening gathered via a closed online website and anonymous group chat to collate materials and prepare for the lawsuit. In many ways, retaining the anonymity of the participants helped the complaint to proceed promptly and smoothly without any issues. The fans decided to trust one another in the closed online website and anonymous group chat, and focused on the tasks in preparation for the complaint. Disclosing any personal information of the organizer or other participants

Figure 13. Text message with group chat link for those who wish to file a complaint against Kang Sung Hoon. Screenshot by Areum Jeong.

could lead to others making suspicious claims about them being connected to Kang or having an agenda against Kang.

The organizer of the lawsuit posted updates about the process on the DCinside community. Although these updates were not detailed for various legal reasons, they provided brief information on the progress of the lawsuit and kept other fans who were not participating in the lawsuit informed. Since it was not possible to join the lawsuit unless one had donated funds to the screening event, other fans provided support by donating funds for the lawyer's fee. The lawyer's fee was raised in a single afternoon, thus showing the fans' fervor and interest in this lawsuit. In addition to the lawsuit, fans also filed a complaint to the Korea Consumer Agency to request a refund of the fan club membership fees.

On December 7, 2018, fans posted another statement urging YG Entertainment to express their position regarding future plans for SECHSKIES.[26] Fans' statement claimed that they could no longer accept Kang's misdemeanors and demanded that YG Entertainment reorganize the group by officially excluding Kang so that not only fans but also other members of the group would not suffer emotional distress. Starting in September 2018, Kang was excluded from all SECHSKIES events, including the October 2018 concert and promotion of newly released merchandise. YG Entertainment produced and released SECHSKIES merchandise which only featured the other four members. Yang Hyun Suk, the head of YG Entertainment, announced that "SECHSKIES will undergo a revamp" and prepare a new album for 2019, but did not comment on Kang. While Kang was accused of several allegations, publicly denouncing an artist who is directly affiliated with the agency could be embarrassing for YG Entertainment.[27]

Finally, on January 1, 2019, YG Entertainment officially announced, in line with mounting fan demands, that Kang would be excluded from all future SECHSKIES activities.[28] Kang himself posted an official statement regarding his position via his fan club website, stating that he was sorry about the fans' "continuous misunderstandings" and apologized to SECHSKIES members and fans for all the distress he caused them. That being said, Kang did not provide any documents or evidence to support his previous claims.

Kang's exclusion from SECHSKIES did not stop the fans' actions, nor did it appease their anger. Fans did not merely organize lawsuits and send requests to YG Entertainment; they were also active in stimulating public discourse on Kang's misdemeanors by emailing news reporters and communicating with TV programs that deal with current events. Several fans even went to the trouble of conducting interviews with such TV programs. *Silhwatamsade* (Truth exploration), a TV program broadcasted by MBC that deals with current events, aired a twenty-five-minute feature on Kang's misdemeanors and the fans' positions on January 30, 2019. Several fans appeared on the program, providing testimonies of Kang's misdemeanors and reasons for their collective actions. The fan club manager's brother also appeared, providing a full account of his sister and Kang's relationship, stating that the two were the only staff members of Hoony World and were living together at that time.[29]

In March 2019, I was able to interview a fan (hereafter, "A"), who appeared on *Silhwatamsade* to provide testimony on Kang's misdemeanors and fans' positions about the situation. A's comments offer insights into an individual experience of taldeok that was part of a broader movement.

Q: What is your relationship to Kang Sung Hoon and SECHSKIES?

A: I have been a fan of SECHSKIES since their debut in 1997. I buy all of their albums and merchandise, attend all concerts and fan meetings, and participate in fan activities such as streaming and voting. I would describe myself as a loyal fan of twenty-two years. However, I am not a fan of Kang anymore. I still support the other members of SECHSKIES, though.

Q: Why did you decide to appear on *Silhwatamsade*?

A: I heard that the program was going to do a feature on Kang and was looking for interviewees. I wanted to share my experiences as a long-time SECHSKIES fan and my suspicions of Kang, and also other fans' positions about the situation. I wanted to share these because I wanted the program to provide a clear picture of Kang's misdemeanors and the current situation. I was worried that the program might show only the tip of the iceberg or sympathize with Kang. And I didn't want the viewers to think the fans were enraged just because Kang and his fan club manager are in a relationship. Fans became angry because Kang lied repeatedly and embezzled funds. By providing these kinds of information, I hoped the program would reveal Kang's deceitful actions and bring attention to the case so Kang would be punished severely later.

Q: What do you think happened?

A: I strongly believe that Kang and his fan club manager embezzled funds and swindled fans and the Taiwanese agency.

Q: Why do you think fans are angry? Why did fans file a lawsuit against Kang?

A: Like I said, I don't think fans were enraged because Kang had a girlfriend. He is almost forty years old! Fans became angry because Kang lied repeatedly about his relationship with his fan club manager and didn't solve the issues regarding fan club management. Fans were also angry because Kang didn't provide any documents or proof to support his claims. All he did was say that he is innocent, and we can't trust him anymore. Right now, it certainly looks like Hoony World embezzled funds. Kang's former fans decided to file a lawsuit to punish Kang and to make sure this lawsuit sets an example for other K-pop artists.

Q: Do you think this shows fans as active agents, trying to reserve their rights?

A: Yes. Unlike how the general public and media view K-pop fans, fans today are not brainwashed teenagers. Most fans are smart and extremely resourceful in utilizing digital media and technology. Fans are not afraid to take action and voice their opinions via social media.

Q: What do you want to say to Kang? What actions do you want him to take?

A: He should take full responsibility for his actions. And I hope he realizes that fans were angered and disappointed by his lies. Although he

> is no longer a member of SECHSKIES, I hope he will stop creating trouble, because whenever he does the media reports him as "a former member of the group SECHSKIES" and I don't want SECHSKIES to be associated with him any longer.

The episode garnered much attention from the press and the general public. While fans were already familiar with the program's contents, many of them noted that it was important to voice their opinions and current position through mainstream media. Although the fans that participated in the collective movement and the lawsuit do not represent the opinion of all SECHSKIES fans, they represent the majority that was angered by Kang's misdemeanors. Moreover, their actions are significant in that they represent K-pop fans who are able to act upon communal goals utilizing critical thinking and careful preparation as well as the communication and discussion resources cultivated in and by online and in-person fandom communities. Their organized actions demonstrate a high-profile manifestation of the collective agency of K-pop fandom activities even when—or perhaps especially when—such activities involve a collective exit from a fandom.

In April 2019, Kang's former fans who filed a complaint with the Korea Consumer Agency received a text message containing a gift card and short message explaining that the gift card was a partial refund of the fan club membership fee. Although Kang was eventually found not guilty on all charges, former fans who believe his past actions to be deceitful view the partial refund as a small victory. Ultimately, this case study illustrates how the exiting deokhu's affective labor can work to materialize greater accountability and reparative action.

Confessions on Exiting Lucas's Fandom

I have my own experience of a deokhu exit. Lucas (Wong Yuk-hei) was a member of K-pop boy group NCT and C-pop boy group WayV, both of which are managed by SM Entertainment. Born in 1999, Lucas made his debut as an NCT member in 2018 and WayV member in 2019. His handsome features, charismatic stage presence, and charming attitude brought him to popularity, eventually helping him become selected as a member of SuperM, SM Entertainment founder Lee Soo-man's ambitious project bringing together some of the best and brightest members from different boy groups, in 2019. Even during the pandemic, Lucas's activities in the K-pop and C-pop sectors did not wane—in fact, he seemed to thrive more

+82 1600-4658

Text Message
Apr 8, 2019 3:33 PM

[Web발신]
[도서문화 1만원권]
8049-2519-3994-1086 2400

죄송하고 감사드립니다
후니월드3기키트

Figure 14. Text message containing digital gift card. Screenshot by Areum Jeong.

than ever. Indeed, in chapter 2, I described my own experiences at fansign events with him during this time. But on August 23, 2021, a scandal erupted that tainted his glittering image and put him on hiatus until April 2024. Lucas was accused by several alleged ex-girlfriends of cheating on, gaslighting, and even leeching money from them.[30]

In the immediate aftermath of the scandal, I observed how fans deal with new information and how assimilating this information could shape their own identities as Lucas fans. Regardless of the veracity of the accusations and whether fans believed them or not, each accusation was shared and translated among fans on social media. While some fans became skeptical about Lucas's character and personality after reading the accusations, other fans flatly denied their veracity, stating that those posting/sharing the accusations were haters or stalkers. Fans seemed divided in their allegiance. Sujeong Kim reminds us that when an idol's moral personality, such as goodness or sincerity, is revealed, the public instantly praises and rewards him or her.[31] The opposite can also happen: The emotional egalitarianism and collective moralistic ethos of Korean society sometimes operate as a violence demanding political correctness by monitoring every action and word of successful celebrities with popularity and wealth. But what is interesting is that fans do not deviate from this public egalitarianism and moralistic ethos. They apply moral standards not only to the idols they don't love, but also to the idols they do love. In particular, this effect on idols is easily expressed by fandom activities via digital platforms and social media, as was the case for Lucas, whose character was closely scrutinized by fans in the wake of these accusations.

Many fans also make videos that include their thoughts on idol scandals, and this happened with Lucas. As discussed in previous chapters, fan-made videos allow fans to center their own personalities and perspectives while creating forums for commentary and connection with other fans. In 2021, a fan video titled "Press Conference of a Retiring Lucas Stan Ft. Bubble Msgs" by Yudeokmo went viral among fan communities.[32] Recorded on a virtual meeting platform, the three young women depict the typical press conference that Korean celebrities hold when they have to make a public statement. Two women, situated on top of the screen, play the role of journalists and the woman on the bottom of the screen portrays a former fan of Lucas. The humorous editing and fan's responses to the journalists' questions made the clip go viral.

"How do you feel?" one of the journalists asks the fan. The fan does not answer but takes a swig of soju from the bottle. "When did you learn about this issue?" The journalist tries again. While explaining the situation when she had learned about Lucas's scandal, the former fan holds her head in her hands and musses her hair in frustration and takes another drink. Then she turns her camera so it shows the posters of Lucas hung on her walls. She gets up and shouts at the posters, but the sound is edited so the viewer assumes that she is swearing at Lucas.

"What will happen to your photo cards?" another journalist asks the fan. "In three days, the [photo card] price plummeted so I decided to keep them. They are memories anyway," the fan says in a weary tone. Because the price of an idol photo card often becomes a criterion in measuring his popularity, the fan's dejection implies that many of Lucas's fans had left the fandom. "Do you have anything to say to him?" the journalist asks. Again, the fan turns to the poster and shouts, which is edited again to suggest profanities. "My memories with him are one-sided of course, but were they all fake? I want to ask if all his words were all fake," she says, looking at the camera.

"Are you retiring from the K-pop idol industry [as a fan]?" a journalist asks. She replies, "He really gave me so much hope and dreams, but they were all fabricated. I cannot trust anyone for now." The journalist asks, "Will you stay firm in your decision whatever handsome idol appears?" The fan looks confused and stammers. For a brief moment, she even looks hopeful: "What kind of . . . handsome idol?" She decides that she is retiring temporarily for now in expectations of a new handsome idol. The reporters then ask to take photos. The fan holds up several photos of Lucas to the camera, showing how much merchandise she had purchased while she was a fan.

"Did you trust and love him?" The fan starts to answer with an exasperated expression: "He was my son! Do you want to see my Bubble?" She voluntarily shares screenshots of the Bubble messages she had sent to Lucas. Her messages are full of affection for the idol: she frequently asks about his health and compliments him on his work. After taking another swig of soju, the fan shows the last message she had sent to Lucas, which was a very lengthy one. This shows that she had been a very devoted fan: When first subscribing to Bubble, the subscriber can only write a few words in a text message, but the length of words increases each month with each subscription. So the fan's lengthy text shows that she had been a paying customer of Bubble for a long time. Her affective labor—consuming Bubble, which profits the industry, and sending affectionate text messages often—is the type that many fans perform every day. In this context, then, deokhu viewers would understand how the extent of the fan's investment and engagement deepened her feelings of frustration and even betrayal.

At the end of the clip, a lengthy text appears in the background, suggesting that the fan is also dealing with feelings of regret and even inadvertent complicity:

> I am sorry I tried to persuade many people to subscribe to Lucas's Bubble. I am sorry I sent you his photos when you didn't care about him. I am sorry I kept sending his photos and clips in group chats when nobody cared. There must have been some people who did not want to see them, so I am sorry for sharing his photos and clips. When asked how I was doing, I am sorry I answered with his well-being, not mine. I am sorry I kept blabbering about him when nobody asked. I won't do that anymore. I will forget about my shameful past and move on with my life.

Much like this fan, many fans feel guilty and sorry when idols misbehave, because they are promoters of these idols. In this way, they show a desire to repair social relationships that have been negatively, even if indirectly, impacted by an idol's behavior.

As a Lucas fan myself, I was devastated and hoped that the accusations were false—simply defamations of some *sasaeng* (stalker fan). Yet, based on my engagements in K-pop activities for more than two decades, I knew that there could also be truth to them. What became a turning point for many fans and myself was SM Entertainment's reaction to the scandal. Previously, SM Entertainment had never released an official statement regarding an idol's personal matters, including relationship issues. (They have, however, released official statements on criminal acts.) Lucas's scandal became the first case in which SM Entertainment released an official statement about an idol's personal life, apologizing for Lucas's actions and announcing his hiatus from all group activities, which shocked many fans. In addition, SM Entertainment decided not to release Lucas and Hendery's upcoming single, which was supposed to drop on August 25, 2021. After weeks of promotion and build-up, the decision to forgo the release of the upcoming single was as shocking as the official statement. To many fans, SM Entertainment's responses to Lucas's scandal, even though they did not reveal any details or comment on the truth of the accusations, indicated that some, if not all, of the accusations were founded on truth. Had it just been a matter of some hater or stalker posting lies on social media, it would not have been difficult for SM Entertainment to pursue legal action to protect their investments in Lucas.

Fans who were on the fence when the first accusation came out seemed to have made up their minds after seeing SM's official statement and decision not to release the new single. Following news of SM's position, many fans closed their fan accounts, posting short statements saying they would no longer support Lucas. Fans who had many followers also became victims of hate from those who chose to stand with Lucas. I underwent a similar experience when I closed my fan account, where I had posted the many fansign videos with Lucas. This fan account had several thousand followers, mostly comprised of Lucas fans. When I posted about leaving the fandom, several fans replied with hateful comments and messages.

In the immediate aftermath of the scandal, I could see that the majority of East Asian fans—fans of Chinese, Japanese, and Korean descent or ethnicity—exited the fandom, whereas fans of other regions continued to support Lucas. While there are a small number of East Asian fans who continue to support Lucas, the size of this demographic in the fandom, and the fandom size overall, shrank dramatically. There was a viral meme that the *yugyo* (Confucian) girls could not tolerate Lucas's behavior and scandal. This corroborates my argument that fans believe there is a certain code of conduct that idols should abide by. And for these fans, Lucas had definitely broken that code.

Advocating for Reflexive Practices on Fanning in Seyeon Oh's *Seongdeok* (*Fanatic*)

"One day, *oppa* became a criminal. I became a failed deokhu." Seyeon Oh's *Seongdeok* (*Fanatic*) is an independent documentary film that traces the director's journey of fanning the now-fallen K-pop star Jung Joon-young, learning about Jung's sexual offenses, and exiting the fandom. The director also interviews fans of other idols who have committed crimes or misdemeanors. The film received favorable reviews from critics and audiences, despite being a low-budget documentary with limited release. It became so popular among K-pop fans that it sold out in a matter of seconds when it was screened at local film festivals in Korea from 2021 to 2022. On social media, many fans shared how the director's and interviewees' thoughts resonated with them. Bringing together multiple realms and modes of active fandom we have discussed—digital fan practices, archiving fan practices, performative video fan practices—this film and its circulation offer a space to reflect on the impact deokhu performances of affective labor can have on the wider culture of K-pop fandom.

Seongdeok, a portmanteau of the Korean words *seonggong* (successful) and *deokhu*, signifies a successful fan. The director viewed herself as a seongdeok of Jung, as she was able to make Jung notice her at fansign events (by attending fan events wearing a traditional Korean dress), eventually appearing on a TV program as a seongdeok who is both Jung's enthusiastic fan and an A-student in high school. But after Jung's activities with the Burning Sun scandal were revealed, the director felt enraged at him, sad that her precious memories were sullied, and also guilty about having been Jung's fan while he was committing atrocious acts against other women.

During these difficult times, the director discussed her conflicting emotions with other fans who were going through similar experiences. Identifying a need for an outlet that would allow communal processing and reflection, she decided that she wanted to make a film that could console K-pop fans who underwent or were undergoing a similar thing. Although the director was an undergraduate student who did not have any prior experience in filmmaking or interviewing, she started shooting stories of herself and other fans. Her unique position as a fan of a fallen idol who empathized with other fans was more than enough to draw heartfelt testimonies from other fans. These fans confessed their *heugyeoksa*, a word which signifies an embarrassing past of fanning someone who is revealed to be a criminal.

The director poses questions that look back at her activities, revealing reflexive practices in K-pop fandom that can inspire but also result from the process of a deokhu exit. The director and her friend, who used to be a Seungri fan, get together to do a "merch funeral" and dispose of their merchandise. They light candles and go over each item one by one before parting with them. They reminisce about what each piece of merchandise represents, summoning the memories of how much they loved their former bias. In the end, the two ex-fans cannot burn or throw the objects away "because of the memories." The ex–Seungri fan remarks, "Before I took out the merch, I hated him so much but now I can't say anything bad. . . . I hate the present-day Seungri, but I didn't back then." Applying Sara Ahmed's idea of how objects, or rather, our relationships with objects, can perform affect, we can say that the K-pop merchandise used in this scene is performative.[33] These objects do not function as insignificant items or materials. Rather, these objects carry the experiences of the fans' memories and happiness, and now, regret and shame. In other words, their significance is now not about their connection to the idol, but about the fan's subjectivity and experiences and the positive memories they have from their fandom experiences.

Several interviewees discuss how they could no longer love someone who harms other women and how they are angry that these idols sullied their happy memories. "Even supporting someone like that feels like a crime, . . . and although he was found not guilty, it should not be dealt [with] lightly and he should recognize the impacts of his actions," one fan says. Another fan remarks that she feels guilty just because she used to be a fan and also feels indirectly associated with her former bias's crimes. Numerous fans experience similar sentiments as seen in online spaces. A Twitter account (@xlqptdudn) posted the following tweet on August 4, 2019: "I worked hard not to sully *oppa*'s name, but why do you [*oppa*] live like that, making me fucking mad?" This tweet, which went viral among Korean users, resurfaces each time an idol commits a crime or misbehaves. After conversing with the interviewees, the director questions, "Are we [fans] victims or oppressors or both?" Although she wants to be free from guilt, she cannot find it in herself to be so. When asked whether she really did not know what kind of person Jung is, she cannot respond right away. Even if she did not know what kind of person he is, the act of not knowing feels like her fault. She feels guilty that the love and support she gave Jung helped afford him the greater influence and power that allowed him to more easily commit his abuses.

The director, who had previously reprimanded a journalist for reporting on Jung's crimes, looks back at her actions and formally apologizes to the journalist. After wondering why some fans continue to support idols who committed crimes, the director visits a rally that supports former President Park Geun-hye, who was impeached and imprisoned during the time the documentary was filmed. This broadens the thematic focus of the film, as it links K-pop to broader structures of power, including state power. The director meets Park's supporters, who enthusiastically explain why Park was "wrongfully imprisoned" and how they want to support her during the current difficult times. Interestingly, in late 2022 when the film was released in theaters, Park was pardoned, and similarly, there continued to be revelations of idols' misbehavior or crimes, which showed that the film focused on a timely relevant subject. Many fans posted on social media that the documentary should be implemented as a required educational resource for K-pop idols and trainees.

In 2022, I attended a screening of this film in Seoul. I noticed that the majority of the audience were young women in their teens and twenties who laughed at or sighed with empathy during particular scenes of the film. After the screening and during the Q & A with the audience, several audience members opened their questions with variations on the introduction "I used to be a fan of X . . . ," and named another fallen idol due guilty of social crimes. Other audience members let out a deep sigh expressing sympathy and commiseration. Indeed, Oh recounted her own experiences as a teenage K-pop fan who was looked down upon while attending fan activities, and felt that this phenomenon of idol's abusing women was ironic when the main consumer demographic of the K-pop industry are young Korean women in their teens and twenties. Through her film, the director wanted to show the multifaceted experiences and emotions of these fans which might be contrary to what others believe. In addition to showcasing the fans' side of the story, she also tries to make sense of what she is feeling after leaving Jung's fandom. Eventually, she encourages fans not to feel guilty about their bias's wrongful deeds and to continue to find (new) love, because it is not the fans' fault, but the faults of the idols and the industry.

During a virtual Q & A session held on April 16, 2024, as part of my Korean Popular Culture course at Arizona State University, Seyeon Oh responded to a student's question about fans forgiving idols for their misdemeanors. In Korean pop culture, she explained, the industry sells the idol's personality as much as—or perhaps even more—than their work. Fans are not just cheering stars from afar; they believe they helped with the star's growth and success, eventually "raising" the star. In such circumstances, fans' desires and expectations toward idols escalated as digital media and technology advanced, as discussed in chapters 1 and 2. Therefore, Korean fans may seem less forgiving than Western fans, since Western fans tend to forgive fallen stars or to separate stars' personal and professional lives.

"Sadly, this film continues to be relevant," the director commented. "Whenever there are incidents, the film becomes viral like a meme. I hope that one day the film won't be needed anymore."

As the director's statement to my class demonstrates, this film resonates with Jungwon Kim's encouragement for fans to take a step beyond boycotting or canceling misbehaving idols to look at how their misdemeanors are connected to the larger entertainment industry, perhaps also including some fanning practices.[34] This reveals that a deokhu exit from an idol's fandom is not always a total exit from deokhu values and performances of fandom organized around the subjectivities and perspectives of actual fan communities. Instead, the creative affective labor being shown here—of attending to the wounds of or healing a (dis)affected fandom—exhibits reflexive forms of mutual care as well as a vision for the wider industry and culture where such interventions "won't be needed anymore."

Conclusion

Drawing from fans' discussions via online communities, interviews, news articles, and social media, this chapter examined fans' collective acts in filing a complaint against former SECHSKIES member Kang Sung Hoon, fans' responses after former NCT/Way member Lucas was accused for inappropriate relationships, and Seyeon Oh's documentary film *Seongdeok* (*Fanatic*) (2021), and analyzed why fans exit the fandom due to idols' misdemeanors while revealing fans' desires and expectations. In addition, this chapter focused on fans' performance in effectively organizing action against idols' corrupt and deceitful actions, showing fans to be active consumers who voice their opinions on matters of ethics and law and mobilize action. Through a close examination of such case studies, this chapter showed how fans' dissatisfaction with the behaviors of their idols directly impacts how they choose to perform deokhu and, perhaps more significantly, choose to performatively exit deokhu.

Examining these recent instances indicates several trends at play that encourage us to consider even deokhu exits as representing another instance of fans performing the *materialization of affective labor* in ways that directly contribute to the workings of K-pop as a fan-centered industry and set of cultural products. In all these instances, we see fans making room for and centering the emotional and material well-being of others who have supported idols and K-pop more broadly yet have experienced harm through these relationships, whether this harm is the economic fallout of an abruptly canceled and unrefunded fan meeting, instances of sexual violence or sexist misbehavior, or feelings of betrayal or personal guilt and shame for having supported an idol who did not uphold community standards.

Epilogue

"Taeyong, I'm so happy to see you again before I leave for the States."

"Are you leaving tomorrow?"

"No, the day after tomorrow."

"To Arizona?"

In the summer of 2023, I attended five in-person fansigns of Taeyong, leader of K-pop group NCT, in promotion of the release of his first solo mini album *SHALALA*. Although I had previously seen him perform live, it was my first time meeting him in person, one-on-one. Before going to the fansigns, I wrote a letter (as gifts were not permitted) and rehearsed what I would say to him at the event. During my conversations with Taeyong, I told him how he had become a source of comfort and strength for me since 2021 and that I was (and still am) infatuated with him. The opportunity to meet and converse with Taeyong brought me great joy. And Taeyong, being the attentive person he is, remembered details from our previous conversations, such as my impending move to Arizona for a new job. When he wished me luck on my new journey, it filled me with happiness.

While attending these in-person fansigns, I noticed that half of the attendees were non-Koreans, even though the events took place in Seoul. When I asked some of these fellow fans, in English, whether they reside in Korea, they told me no. Many non-Korean fans, they elaborated, would visit Korea when their favorite idol dropped a new album. During the two-week promotion period, many of these foreign fans would get together, reserving an Airbnb or hotel room together to save costs, and sharing information on how to participate in fan events. They would then often attend these events together. After our conversation, I noticed that many vendors selected an equal number of Korean and non-Korean fans at fansign events. This kind of policy would make both Korean and foreign fans feel "seen." And acknowledging their presence fairly in fan events might encourage more non-Korean fans to participate in K-pop events, and of course also consume and promote K-pop.

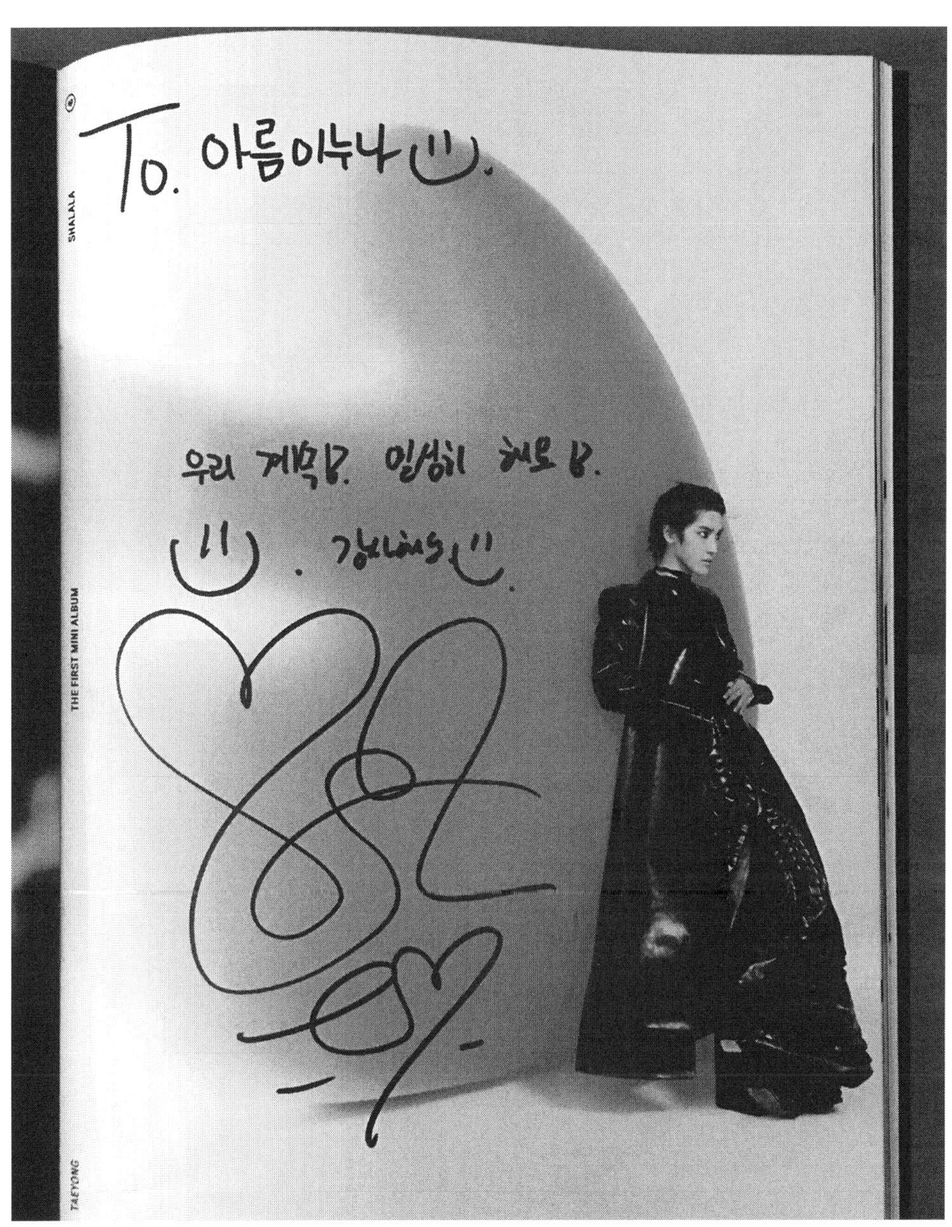

Figure 15. Taeyong's autograph. Photo by Areum Jeong.

Perhaps it is impossible to be a K-pop fan without contributing to the neoliberal and capitalist structures of the industry in some way—album purchases, concert tickets, event costs, social media subscriptions, even international plane trips all add up, making fandom a time- and money-intensive pursuit that is more accessible to some individuals than to others. It is also hard not to see the ways that K-pop industry structures can still perpetuate patterns of devaluing or undercompensating affective labor that tends to remain gendered and racialized. This is the case even as many K-pop fans experience burn out or exhaustion.

As an academic who is also a fan, I have myself sometimes wrestled with the industry's inequalities, contradictions, and tolls. But this wrestling, as we saw in previous chapters, may itself be seen as a form of affective labor.

Maybe fanning responsibly means doing the labor of fully acknowledging the paradoxes of the industry and being reflexive about one's own actions. Heera Oh's revised publication, *Gwamorip deokhureul wihan taldeok annaeseo* (Exit guide for deeply immersed fans), mirrors my own processes of reengaging with fandom activities as I question how to be "a good fan" and reconfigure my role as a responsible consumer.[1]

While prioritizing the responsibilities of my new position as Assistant Professor of Korean Studies at Arizona State University, including the writing of this book, I found time to keep up with fan activities in fall 2023 when NCT U released the *Golden Age* album and when NCT 127 released the *Fact Check* album, and into Spring 2024 when Taeyong released his second solo mini album, *TAP*. I went to KCON Los Angeles to see Taeyong's performance on August 18, 2023, flew to Seoul to attend NCT 127's THE UNITY concert on November 26, 2023, and to see Taeyong's first solo concert, TY TRACK, on February 24 and 25, 2024.

In addition, I attended twenty-one video call fansigns with Taeyong from October 2023 to March 2024. Due to the time difference, these video calls always took place around 3 or 4 a.m. in Arizona. But talking to Taeyong always gave me great comfort and energy that sustained me during the hectic semester, and motivated me to finish this project. And video calls gave me the opportunity to show Taeyong objects or visual materials, which was not permitted during in-person fansigns. I was able to give him a virtual tour of my new office (which basically looks like a Taeyong shrine), the Phoenix Herpetological Society (because Taeyong is a fan of reptiles), and the Seattle Aquarium (because of their special exhibition in collaboration with Nintendo's *Animal Crossing: New Horizons* game, of which Taeyong is a fan).

In addition, by documenting and uploading excerpts of my video calls on social media, I was able to promote Taeyong's activities and converse with

Figure 16. Inside the venue of Taeyong's concert. Photo by Areum Jeong.

other fans. And in July 2024, I was able to meet many of these new virtual friends in Seoul to celebrate Taeyong's birthday. On this trip, I co-organized a photo exhibition/*saengka* and an in-person gathering for Taeyong fans.

Although Taeyong had enlisted for mandatory military service on April 15, 2024, and would not "active" again in the K-pop industry until the end of 2025, fans celebrated his birthday by reminiscing about their happy moments with him.

Researching and writing about the shifting discourses and practices of K-pop fandom felt cathartic and also helped me make sense of my fan activities. I had often felt conflicted about how the neoliberal capitalist industry materialized my and other fans' labor of love and performance of care, but I have also fully witnessed how fandom labor can alter or push structures by producing meaning and value through individual development, collective sociality, and advocating for cultural and social change.

K-pop fan activities today, more than ever, are complex and labor-intensive. In mainstream fan spaces, which are often where fans cultivate

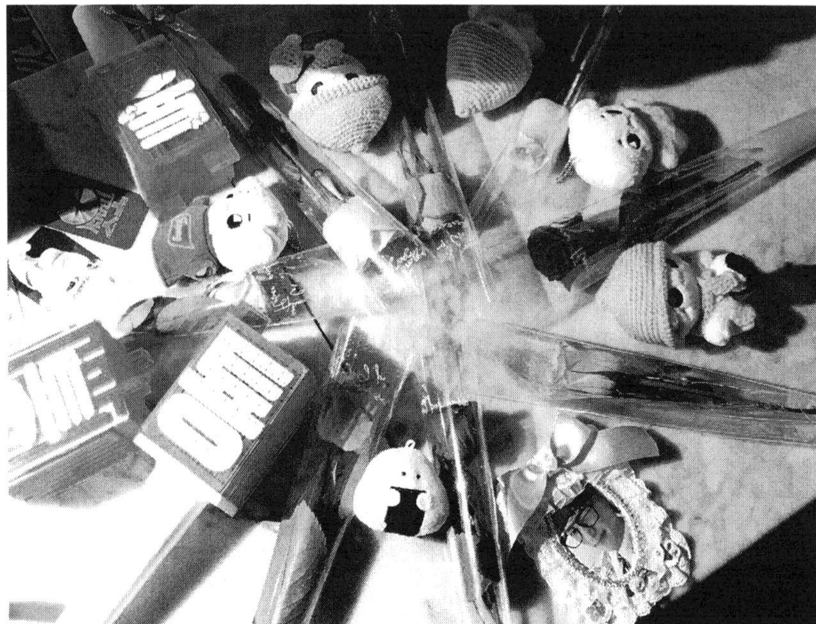

Figure 17. Taking a photo with other Taeyong fans after Taeyong's concert. Photo by Areum Jeong.

their love of K-pop, loyalty is performed primarily through digital engagements that promote and produce profit for the industry. Yet digital labor in K-pop fandoms also, significantly, creates kinship between far-flung fans and facilitates the formation of diverse communities that are more than merely markets. Fan-made videos also reveal a shift in focus from centering the idols to centering the fans themselves, who are often young women, but span a range of gender identities, sexualities, and ages. Notably, this has shifted some of the compensation structures of K-pop fandom practices, as some fans monetize their labor in various ways. Through the affective labor of performing fan identity, fans construct representations of themselves while also helping to shape norms and expectations around what constitutes desirable relational dynamics in K-pop.

While K-pop fandom is often highly mediated by commercial digital platforms, it also takes place in and through individual fans' production and consumption of archival materials documenting aspects of fandom that fans express as important to themselves personally and communally. Memoirs and photo exhibitions, as we have seen, are places where fans define themselves as cocreators of K-pop's meanings. Themes they center in these kinds

Figure 18. Screenshot of video call with Taeyong. Screenshot by Areum Jeong.

of documents include K-pop as a site of genuine love and bonding (especially among fans); K-pop fandom as driven by agential fans with capacities for self-reflection and critique; and K-pop as a site of personal development and transformation, and also perhaps for incubating social change. Therefore, these are essential realms and practices through which fans give meaning to and strengthen relationships with K-pop, with themselves, and with each other.

Lastly, affective labor is organized toward acts of resistance or enforcing accountability, as well as the operative processes in which fans exit fandoms. Focusing on fans' experiences of exiting fandoms due to idols' misdemeanors and advocacy for reflexive practices in fanning, I analyzed how collective fan activities mobilized to enact change in the industry or impose accountability on performers can heighten fans' sense of agency. This reveals how fans seek

Figure 19. Screenshot of video call with Taeyong. Screenshot by Areum Jeong.

to materialize their own desires and expectations in K-pop, including codes of conduct that are expected from idols. From my perspective as a researcher, over the last decade, fans' deepening critical engagements with K-pop and their efforts to hold the industry accountable to certain fan values has materialized noticeable changes in the industry, from fans campaigning for more environmentally sustainable practices to calling out and boycotting idols who committed gender crimes. Each time, the fans' labor in supporting these causes exceeded my expectations in terms of intensity and impact. And more recently, I witnessed, once again, how K-pop fans create significant changes beyond the K-pop industry.

At 10:30 p.m. on December 3, 2024, former South Korean President Yoon Suk Yeol declared emergency martial law, arguing that it was necessary to protect the country from "anti-state" forces and "falling into ruin." This

Figure 20. Photography exhibition within cup sleeve event celebrating Taeyong's birthday. Photo by Areum Jeong.

was the first martial law declared in South Korea since a coup installed a military dictatorship in 1980. Immediately after Yoon declared martial law, opposition lawmakers rushed to the National Assembly and voted unanimously in favor of lifting the martial law. During this time, protestors also gathered outside the National Assembly to call for Yoon's impeachment. On social media spaces, Koreans shared what was going on in real-time. In addition to charting the unfolding events, they posted responses of anger and disbelief toward Yoon's self-coup, anxiety and concern for the lawmakers and protestors at the scene, and trauma as the martial law declaration dredged up painful memories for those who had experienced authoritarianism during the 1980s or other kinds of disastrous event in which the Korean government did not prioritize the well-being and safety of the people, such as the 2014 *Sewol* ferry disaster or the 2022 Itaewon crowd crush.

In the immediate days after the martial law was lifted, numerous Koreans took to the streets to protest against Yoon and call for his resignation. There are long traditions of both activism and suppression of dissent in Korea. From protests against Syngman Rhee's authoritarianism in the 1960s and Chun Doo-hwan's declaration of martial law in the 1970s and 1980s, to when the Korean people took to the streets from late 2016 to early 2017, the Korean people have routinely mobilized to enact change at the highest levels of power. When the Park Geun-hye administration ushered in a neo-authoritarian regime that attempted to censor Koreans and prevent demonstrations, Koreans responded with creativity and defiance, using digital media to avoid government censorship and organizing mass collective actions. Koreans marched the streets holding candles and these luminous street protests captured nationwide attention and spread. A sea of yellow candlelight became the representative image associated with these protests.

But in the recent protests against Yoon, the scenery has become more colorful. In addition to the yellow lights, various hues of red, orange, green, purple, and white lights dotted the protest crowds, because K-pop fans took their fan club light sticks to the streets. These K-pop light sticks, which range from $30 to $50, represent each fandom and are used to cheer idols during concerts or music TV programs. Fans' collective use of light sticks at concerts and fan events creates a sense of community and connectivity.[2] These light sticks serve as a material and visual representation of fans' love toward their idols and fandom. However, in such special circumstances, these light sticks served another purpose—they served as a visible representation of K-pop fans' engagement with politics.

This was not a wholly new phenomenon. Scholars such as Jungwon Kim examined how K-pop fans' previous participation in the 2016–17 protests against the Park administration diversified Korean protest culture visually and sonically, adding various colors to the protest with light sticks and including K-pop songs to the well-known protests songs.[3] Again in 2024, the different sizes, shapes, and intensity and the versatility of these light sticks represented the fans both individually and collectively. Many Koreans in the streets and online cheered on K-pop fans' active participation in the protests, welcoming their presence with the multicolored and differently shaped light sticks. Some fans created stickers that said "IMPEACH" in Korean and shared them with others to attach to their own light sticks. The anxious and somber protest scene transformed into a cheerful and encouraging mood due to the fans and their colorfully lighted protest. The fans' visibility in the protest crowds moved the Korean people, giving them hope in the younger generation who were not shy to voice their opinions and fight for democracy. In contrast to the ageist and gendered assumptions that generally follow K-pop fans, this was a moment in which fans were accepted and even praised for their democratic actions and the creative ways they stood in solidarity with the Korean people.

In addition to participating in protests, numerous K-pop fans also paid for coffee or food at coffee shops and restaurants in advance near the protest sites. They posted on their social media platforms to gift these refreshments to those participating in protests. "I pre-paid for 100 cups of coffee under [K-pop idol's name] at X coffee shop near the National Assembly subway station. Please help yourself to some coffee!" fans announced. Many participants uploaded photos of coffee and food they received from K-pop fans on social media as a gesture of appreciation. This kind of act aligns with the practice of exchanging or gifting products among fans as discussed in previous chapters while also showing new political horizons of this labor.

During and after protests, numerous K-pop fans, whether they supported the same idol or not, took photos and videos together with their colorful light sticks shining brightly against the dark sky and posted them on social media. These fans were happy to find other fans who supported both K-pop and the same political cause. There were also numerous social media posts by protestors who requested to take a photos and videos with K-pop fans and their light sticks out of awe and surprised delight. Immediately after these protests, Korean news media reported on young women's, especially K-pop fans', powerful impact on the impeachment protests and how it would change Korea's protest scene for a new generation.

While many Koreans were newly informed about K-pop fans and their practices, these K-pop fans, as Korean citizens and members of communities, have consistently been active leaders and players in activism and political campaigns in and beyond Korea. K-pop fan practices spill beyond the borders of the neoliberal capitalist industry to support causes they find important and necessary. For many K-pop fans, not only the music and stars but also their fellow fan communities are at the center of their everyday life, and they remain so when they participate in acts such as large-scale protests. The media's response to and discourse surrounding K-pop fans' participation in the protests shows how we are still far from recognizing K-pop practices as materializing affective labor that may support the K-pop industry but that also has the potential to drive broader societal changes. Furthermore, such ageist and sexist assumptions also downplay or erase the earlier participation of young Korean women in activism and politics.

By identifying and analyzing an efflorescence of fan activities from collective and communal fan activities to decentralized, personalized labor that represents individual fans' personalities and performances of care, this book reveals how K-pop fans, in performing a materialization of affective labor, shape not only K-pop's explosive popularity, but also its cultural and social impacts, cultural politics, and horizons of possibility. As of this writing (May 2025), the long-term effects that K-pop fans will have on Korean politics are beyond the scope of this book. But one thing is certain: fans' affective labor fiercely supports what they love and believe in, and they persevere through hardship using their highly networked and organized communities and reflexive practices to create change and possibilities, in the K-pop industry and beyond. That is the power of K-pop fandom labor.

Notes

Introduction

1. In her research on "comfort women" activism in South Korea and the diaspora, Elizabeth W. Son analyzes memorials and how the materiality of the memorials elicits "performance of care"—embodied acts that materialize concern and interest by providing for the needs of or looking after what one is caring for. Inspired by Son, my work illustrates examples of how K-pop fans' affective labor elicits embodied engagements and performances of care that have been less examined. See Son, *Embodied Reckonings*.

2. Hardt and Negri, *Multitude*, 108.

3. Ahmed, *Cultural Politics of Emotion*, 253.

4. Stanfill and Condis, "Fandom and/as Labor."

5. Kim, *From Factory Girls to K-Pop Idol Girls*, xix.

6. Conquergood, "Rethinking Ethnography"; Madison, *Acts of Activism*.

7. *Merriam-Webster Dictionary*, "otaku," Merriam-Webster, accessed July 15, 2024, https://www.merriam-webster.com/dictionary/otaku

8. Kim, *K-Pop Live*, 16.

9. Kim, "Introduction: Korean Media in a Digital Cosmopolitan World," 8.

10. Galbraith, "'Idols' in Japan, Asia and the world," 203.

11. Galbraith, "'Idols' in Japan, Asia and the world," 202.

12. Galbraith, "'Idols' in Japan, Asia and the world," 208.

13. Aoyagi, *Islands of Eight Million Smiles*.

14. Aoyagi, *Islands of Eight Million Smiles*, 3.

15. Aoyagi, *Islands of Eight Million Smiles*, 16, 72–73, 204.

16. Jung and Lee, "Fandom Managing Stars."

17. Kim, "Sosyeol wep sidae paendeom munhwaui byeonhwa" [Dynamics of Fandom].

18. Choi and Maliangkay, *K-Pop: The International Rise*, 9–10.

19. Cho, "3 Ways That BTS and Its Fans Are Redefining Liveness."

20. King-O'Riain, "'They Were Having So Much Fun, So Genuinely.'"

21. McLaren and Jin, "You Can't Help But Love Them," 100.

22. Shin, "Queer Eye for K-Pop Fandom"; Kwon, *Straight Korean Female Fans and Their Gay Fantasies*; Baudinette, "Idol Shipping Culture," 249–64.

23. Lee, "Of the Fans, by the Fans, for the Fans," 108–32; Ko and Yang, "Namseong aidol geurubui yeoseonghyeomo nollangwa yeoseong paendeomui bunyeol" [Korean Boy Group's Misogyny and Division Between Female Fandom].

24. Kim and Kim, "Haedok paereodaimeul neomeo suhaeng paereodaimeuro" [From Interpretation Paradigm to Performance Paradigm].

25. Horton and Wohl, "Mass Communication and Para-Social Interaction."

26. Chung and Cho, "Fostering Parasocial Relationships with Celebrities on Social Media."

27. Groszman, "Revisiting Parasocial Theory in Fan Studies."

28. Rachel Kowert and Emory Daniel Jr., "One-and-a-Half Sided Parasocial Relationship," 5–6.

29. Areum Jeong, "How the Pyŏnsa Stole the Show."

30. Kim, *From Factory Girls to K-Pop Idol Girls*, xxi.

31. Kim, *From Factory Girls to K-Pop Idol Girls*, xxii.

32. Although it is unclear when the very first Korean celebrity fan club formed, one of the earliest and most popular ones is that of singer Nam Jin, which started with approximately 1,000 members on June 18, 1972. Nam's fan club had a membership fee of 500 won and a monthly membership fee of 100 won, but later grew to approximately 10,000 members. The fan club members sent postcards to broadcasting stations to request Nam's new songs when they were released and also sent postcards as a group for fan voting at the year-end awards ceremony. Attending and applauding at concerts was also a communal activity. As a reciprocal gesture to his fans' support, Nam held a fan event at Nami Island in 1972. This fan meeting was the first fan club event recorded in Korea. "At that time, it was a spectacular sight to see fans arriving in dozens of chartered buses," Nam reminisces in an interview. Fellow celebrities Yi Sang-yeol, Taewon, Yi Tae-shin, Yim Hi-suk, Chams, and An Il, all of whom were close friends, accompanied the event, and it was held in the format of a luxurious mini-show. It was an extravagant outing that included a singing contest by fans, a go-go festival, etc., as well as a lucky draw where fifty people were awarded a solo album signed by Nam as a prize. See Gim, "Gimhyeongchanui daejungeumak iyagi; Yun, *Modeun hyeonjaeui sijak* [Beginning of everything present].

33. Yun, *Modeun hyeonjaeui sijak* [Beginning of everything present], 102.

34. Yun, *Modeun hyeonjaeui sijak* [Beginning of everything present], 103.

35. Yun, *Modeun hyeonjaeui sijak* [Beginning of everything present], 104.

36. To read more on transnational labor, see Koskinen, *Translation and Affect*; Baruch, "Transnational Fandom"; Tamar Herman, "Unpaid Labor of K-Pop Fan Translation Twitter."

Chapter 1

1. Kang, "Yeonghwa 'seongdeok' daedam" [Film *Seongdeok* interview 3 evolving].

2. For a broader picture on how Korean digital platforms and relevant cultures have evolved since the mid-1990s, see "How Korea's Digital Platforms Have Been Evolved?" in Kim and Jin, *Korea's Platform Empire*.

3. "Hallyu 2.0: Seung-Ah Lee," Nam Center for Korean Studies, University of Michigan, accessed March 8, 2022, https://ii.umich.edu/ncks/news-events/events/conferences---symposia/hallyu-2-0--the-korean-wave-in-the-age-of-social-media/hallyu-program/hallyu-2-0--seung-ah-lee.html. Also see Lee, "Of the Fans, by the Fans, for the Fans."

4. "Hallyu 2.0: Seung-Ah Lee."

5. Interview with author in Seoul, Korea, July 2023.

6. Fedorenko, "Idol Ads in the Seoul Metro," 492.

7. Such fan activities are not limited to K-pop, as Thomas Baudinette discusses in his research on Thai BL fandom. According to Baudinette, Thai BL fans' participation in the "strategic manipulation of hashtags online" echo those of K-pop fans who actively utilize social media to promote their biases. Thus, it is not just K-pop idols being exported; K-pop fandom activities are being exported and localized as well. See Baudinette, "Sharing Intimacies," 116–17.

8. "V-LIVE – Star Live App." *Google Play*. Accessed August 18, 2018. https://play.google.com/stre/apps/details?id=com.naver.vapp

9. Lee, "Chinmilhwansangui jakdong bangsik" [How the Intimacy Fantasy Works].

10. Jung, "K-Pop, Indonesian Fandom, and Social Media."

11. King-O'Riain, "'They Were Having So Much Fun, So Genuinely'"; Kim, *K-Pop Live*.

12. Kim, "Sosyeol wep sidae paendeom munhwaui byeonhwa" [Dynamics of Fandom].

13. Scholars who have examined how fans of the popular audition TV program *Produce 101, Season 2* formed imaginary relationships with their idols argue that the affect in the fandom encouraged fans to form communities and engage in affective labor. See Kang et al., "20dae yeoseong paendeomui gamjeong gujowa munhwa silcheon" [Affective Structure and Cultural Practice of Fandom]." Shin-kyu Kang and Jun Hyung Lee view this affective labor to be a mix of play and work as they apply Julian Kücklich's idea of "playbor" in examining the fandom of *Produce 48* in their research. See Kang and Lee, "Saengsangwa sobi sai, noriwa nodong sai" [Between Producing and Consuming]."

14. Cho, "3 Ways That BTS and Its Fans Are Redefining Liveness."

15. McLaren and Jin, "You Can't Help But Love Them," 100.

16. Chang and Park, "Fandom of Hallyu, a Tribe in the Digital Network Era," 270–71.

17. Kim, "Nyumidieo sidaeui paendeomgwa munhwamaegaeja" [Fandom and New Cultural Intermediary in New Media Era], 378–91; Lie, "Sosyeol midieo sahoeyeongyeolseongui paendeom gongdongche hyeongseonge gwanhan tamsaekjeok yeongu" [How Does the Social Connectivity of Social Media Build a Fandom Community?]

18. Galbraith and Karlin, *Idols and Celebrity in Japanese Media Culture*, 107.

19. Galbraith and Karlin, *Idols and Celebrity in Japanese Media Culture*, 108–9.

20. An, *Mangseorineun sarang* [Hesitating love], 108–9.

21. Kim and Kim, "Jipdanjeok dodeokjuui etoseu" [Ethos of Collective Moralism]."

22. Kim and Kim, "Jipdanjeok dodeokjuui etoseu" [Ethos of Collective Moralism], 23.

23. Kim and Kim, "Jipdanjeok dodeokjuui etoseu" [Ethos of Collective Moralism], 24.

24. Kim, "Paendeomgwa peminijeumui jou" [When Fandom Meets Feminism], 72.

25. Kang, "Keipab aidorui japil sagwamun: songeulssiui jinjeongseonggwa paendeomui sobija jeongcheseong" [Handwritten Apologies of K-Pop Idols]."

26. Kang, "Keipab aidorui japil sagwamun," 41.

27. Herman, "Big Hit Entertainment Credits BTS's Success."

28. Choe, "Eumwon aep choegangja mellon" [Melon, the strongest music app].

29. No, "Aidol paendeul nalbam saeumyeo 'eumwon jibungkik'" [Idol fans stay up all night and "kick the roof of the music charts"].

30. *The Show*, SBS Medianet, accessed August 20, 2024, https://programs.sbs.co.kr/sbsm/theshow/main

31. *Show Champion*, MBC PLUS, accessed August 20, 2024, https://m.mbcplus.com/web/program/contentList.do?programInfoSeq=67

32. *M Countdown*, Mnet, accessed August 20, 2024, https://www.mnetplus.world/community/main?communityId=PzfktaFfF9GXMF1CBSnUO

33. *Music Bank*, KBS, accessed August 20, 2024, https://program.kbs.co.kr/2tv/enter/musicbank/pc/index.html

34. *Show! Music Core*, MBC, accessed August 20, 2024, https://program.imbc.com/musiccore

35. *Inkigayo*, SBS, accessed August 20, 2024, https://programs.sbs.co.kr/enter/gayo/main

36. Zhang and Negus, "East Asian Pop Music Idol Production," 2.

37. Sun, "K-Pop Fan Labor and an Alternative Creative Industry," 389.

38. Choi, "Chart Manipulation and Fan Labor," 45.

39. Bonfils, "Search Marketing Guide to Naver."

40. Ji-eun Choe, "2016yeonui aidol paendeom" [Idol Fandom of 2016].

41. Lee and Kao, "'Make It Right.'" To learn more about the ways in which K-pop fans utilize digital strategies to support political causes, see the following essays in *Bangtan Remixed: A Critical BTS Reader*: Octaviany, "Break the Structure"; Atis et al., "From Purple to Pink"; Keskin and Binark, "Yoongi, Can You Hear Me?"

Chapter 2

1. Gang, "[ASMR] VIDEOCALL with yeongtongpaenssa hugi."

2. Chu, "Poseuteu korona keipap aidol paendeurui gamjeong jageobe gwanhan yeongu" [Emotional Work of K-Pop Idol Fans]; J. Kim, *Eumagillyuhakjaui keipapagi [Ethnomusicologist's K-Popping]*.

3. See Kim, *Eumagillyuhakjaui keipapagi*; Lee, "Keipabui segyehwawa dijiteolhwa" [Digitalization and Globalization of K-Pop]"; Magoncia, "OMG! Reaction Videos on YouTube"; Oh, "From Seoul to Copenhagen"; Oh, "Queering Spectatorship in K-Pop"; Oh and Oh, "White-Expat-Fans' Performing K-Pop Other on YouTube"; Oh, "Black K-Pop Fan Videos and Polyculturalism"; Oh, "Korean Wave| K-Pop Fans React," 18; Springman, "'It's Army Versus the U.S. Army'"; Swan, "Transnational Identities and Feeling in Fandom."

4. Oh, "From Seoul to Copenhagen," 29.

5. Yi, "Haibu, aidol paensainhoeseo sogotgeomsa" [HYBE checks underwear at idol fansign].

6. Kim, *Eumagillyuhakjaui keipapagi*, 165–66.

7. Lee and Ji, "Paendeom naeui gyecheung gubyeore daehan yeongu" [Study on Discrimination Inside Fandom in Korea], 26.

8. Puzar and Hong, "Korean Cuties," 333.

9. Puzar and Hong, "Korean Cuties," 337.

10. Puzar and Hong, "Korean Cuties," 347.

11. Epstein and Turnbull, "Girls' Generation?," 319.

12. Kim, "Aidol yukseong peurogeuraem" [Idol Fostering Program], 294.

13. Mabokpil, YouTube, https://www.youtube.com/channel/UC7MQxkON_yXQjJv60hBIW1w/featured

14. Kang, "Aelbeomkkangui gippeumgwa seulpeum" [Ups and downs of album unboxing], 93.

15. Kim, "Home and Homma in K-Pop Fandom."

16. Kim, "Home and Homma in K-Pop fandom," 7–8.

17. Kpop4planet, accessed August 20, 2024, https://www.kpop4planet.com/

Chapter 3

1. Baudinette, "Idol Shipping Culture."

2. An, *Mangseorineun sarang* [Hesitating Love], 44.

3. Lee and Ji, "Paendeom naeui gyecheung gubyeore daehan yeongu" [Study on Discrimination Inside Fandom in Korea], 26.

4. Zhong, "Hommaui paendeom saengsanhwaldongeul tonghaeseo jomyeonghan hommaui yeokalgwa nodongui munhwajeok hamui" [Study on the Cultural Implications of Homema's Role and Labor]," 68–69.

5. Kim, *Eumagillyuhakjaui keipapagi*, 200.

6. Kompare, "Fan Curators and Gateways into Fandom," 107.

7. Kompare, "Fan Curators and Gateways into Fandom," 108.

8. Herman, "K-Pop Fan Meet-Ups in Hong Kong."

9. Hills, "Returning to 'Becoming-a-Fan' Stories," 10.

10. Deobeulyuar, *Bangtansonyeondan anpadeon gwageoui na jonna bulssanghada* [How fucking unfortunate I was when I didn't stan BTS], 45.

11. Debeulyuar, *Bangtansonyeondan anpadeon gwageoui na jonna bulssanghada* [How fucking unfortunate I was when I didn't stan BTS], 65.

12. Laffan, "Positive Psychosocial Outcomes and Fanship in K-Pop Fans," 1.

13. Jin and Yoon, "Social Mediascape of Korean Pop Culture; Laffan, "Positive Psychosocial Outcomes and Fanship in K-Pop Fans."

14. Team Nunaz, *Oneurui halil: bangtan* [To do list: BTS], 171.

15. Team Nunaz, *Oneurui halil: bangtan* [To do list: BTS], 97.

16. Team Nunaz, *Oneurui halil: bangtan* [To do list: BTS], 97–98.

17. Cho, "3 Ways That BTS and Its Fans Are Redefining Liveness."

18. King-O'Riain, "'They Were Having So Much Fun, So Genuinely,'" 16–17.

19. Kim et al., *Bumping into BTS*, 41–43.

20. Kim et al., *Bumping into BTS*, 105.

21. Kim et al., *Bumping into BTS*, 153.

22. For new academic collections of works offering in-depth analyses based on personal experiences, see Ahn et al., *Bangtan Remixed*.

23. Oh, *Naneun naui paeni doellaeyo* [I want to be a fan of myself]; Oh, *Gwamorip deokhureul wihan taldeok annaeseo* [Exit guide for deeply immersed fans].

24. Email interview with author, February 2023.

25. Oh, *Naneun naui paeni doellaeyo* [I want to be a fan of myself], 7–8.

26. Oh, *Gwamorip deokhureul wihan taldeok annaeseo* [Exit guide for deeply immersed fans], https://brunch.co.kr/@0hheera/13

27. Oh, *Gwamorip deokhureul wihan taldeok annaeseo* [Exit guide for deeply immersed fans], https://brunch.co.kr/@0hheera/12

28. Oh, *Gwamorip deokhureul wihan taldeok annaeseo* [Exit guide for deeply immersed fans], https://brunch.co.kr/@0hheera/14

29. Oh, *Gwamorip deokhureul wihan taldeok annaeseo* [Exit guide for deeply immersed fans], https://brunch.co.kr/@0hheera/18

30. Oh, *Gwamorip deokhureul wihan taldeok annaeseo* [Exit guide for deeply immersed fans], https://brunch.co.kr/@0hheera/23

31. Lee, *Hwansangtong* [Phantom Pain], 193–200.

32. Lee, *Hwansangtong* [Phantom Pain], 10. Translated by Rachel Min Park in *Korean Literature Now* 47 (Spring 2020), March 16, 2020, https://klwave.or.kr/klw/magazines/263/articleView.do

33. Lee, *Hwansangtong* [Phantom Pain], 11–12. Translated by Rachel Min Park.

34. For a broader picture of K-pop tourism, see "K-Star Road: Making Gangnam into a K-Pop—Filled Place" in Oh, *Pop City*; and Oh, "Following the Footsteps of BTS."

35. King-O'Riain, "They Were Having So Much Fun, So Genuinely," 1.

36. Lee, *Hwansangtong* [Phantom Pain], 10. Translated by Rachel Min Park.

37. Lee, *Hwansangtong* [Phantom Pain], 11. Translated by Rachel Min Park.

38. For more scholarship on how K-pop fans have become producers of items and services consumed by other fans, see Saeji, "Making Icons."

Chapter 4

1. Click, *Anti-Fandom*, 5.

2. Click, *Anti-Fandom*, 5.

3. Click, *Anti-Fandom*, 3.

4. Jenkins, *Textual Poachers*; Lori Kido Lopez, "Fan-Activists and the Politics of Race"; Hinck, "Ethical Frameworks and Ethical Modalities"; Jenkins and Shresthova, "Up, Up, and Away!"

5. Choi, "K-Pop Idols: Media Commodities," 149.

6. Kim and Kim, "Jipdanjeok dodeokjuui etoseu" [Ethos of Collective Moralism]."

7. Berbiguier and Younghan Cho, "Keipabui hanguk paendeome daehan yeongu: haeoe paendeure daehan insigeul jungsimeuro" [Understanding the Korean Fandom of K-Pop]."

8. Eunkyo Kang, "Yeonghwa *Seongdeok* daedam 3" [Film *Seongdeok* Interview 3].

9. Han, "Stars' Fans Become Smart Shareholders."

10. "Hallyu 2.0: Seung-Ah Lee," Nam Center for Korean Studies, University of Michigan, accessed March 8, 2022, https://ii.umich.edu/ncks/news-events/events/conferences---symposia/hallyu-2-0--the-korean-wave-in-the-age-of-social-media/hallyu-program/hallyu-2-0--seung-ah-lee.html. Also see Lee, "Of the Fans, by the Fans, for the Fans."

11. Tamar Herman, "Blackpink Fans Protest YG Entertainment."

12. 그래 넌 최고의 여자, 갑질
so 존나게 잘해 갑질
아 근데 생각해보니 갑이었던 적 없네
갑 떼고 임이라 부를게 임질 ('농담')
여자는 최고의 선물이야 ('호르몬 전쟁')

can be translated into:

> Yes, you're the best woman, abuse of power [or "best vagina" as *gap* may signify "best" and *jil* can signify "vagina"]

so fucking good at it, abuse of power
But when I think about it, you never were powerful
So I will take off power and call you dear, gonorrhea [from *Joke*]
Women are the best gift [from *War of Hormone*]

Hui-yoon Yim, "'Bangtansonyeondan oppadeul, yeohyeomieyo?'" ["BTS oppas, are you hating on women?"].

13. Yi, "Bangtansonyeondan" [BTS issues official apology].

14. Bicker, "Gangnam"; August Brown, "K-Pop's Innocent Image."

15. Victoria Kim, "K-Pop's K-Porn Problem."

16. CedarBough T. Saeji, "Seungri Scandal."

17. Se-yeon O (Seyeon Oh), *Seongdeok* [Fanatic].

18. Benjamin, "Classic K-Pop boy band SECHSKIES."

19. Gang, "Gangseonghun, daeman konseoteu chwiso" [Kang Sung Hoon cancels concert in Taiwan].

20. Han, "Gangseonghun paenkeulleop Assi" [Kang Sung Hoon fan club's A].

21. Gim, "'Daeman paenmiting sagi piso'" ["Taiwan fan meeting fraud accused"].

22. Gim, "Gangseonghun, daeman paenmiting gwallyeon YG" [Kang Sung Hoon, issue of illegally using YG].

23. Gim, "Deung dollin paendeom" [Fandom turns its back on Kang Sung Hoon].

24. Gang, "Gangseonghun paendeul, haemyeongyoguseo balpyo" [Kang Sung Hoon fans issue a request for explanation].

25. Gang, "Gangseonghun gosohan paendeul" [Fans who sued Kang Sung Hoon].

26. Gim, "'YG, jekki jaejeongbi ipjang pyomyeonghara'" ["YG, express your position on SECHSKIES"].

27. Gim, "Hae neomgineun gangseonghun 'ipjang balpyo'" [Kang Sung Hoon's "position announcement" as the year passes].

28. Jang, "YG cheuk 'gangseonghungwa jeonsokgyeyak haeji, apeurodo jal doegil baranda'" [YG, "We have terminated our exclusive contract with Kang Sung Hoon and wish him well"].

29. Choe, "Gangseonghun aein oppa" [Kang Sung Hoon's lover's brother].

30. Dong, "NCT Member Lucas Goes on Hiatus."

31. S. Kim, "Paendeomgwa peminijeumui jou" [When Fandom Meets Feminism], 72.

32. Yudeokmo, "Press Conference of a Retiring Lucas Stan."

33. Ahmed, "Happy Objects," 33.

34. Kim, *Eumagillyuhakjaui keipapagi*, 243.

Epilogue

1. Heera Oh, *Gwamorip deokhureul wihan taldeok annaeseo* [Exit guide for deeply immersed fans].

2. Herman, "Communality of K-Pop Lightsticks," *Notes on K-Pop*, November 14, 2022, https://notesonkpop.com/the-communality-of-k-pop-lightsticks/; Lee and Kao, "'I Need U.'"

3. Jungwon Kim, "'With the Brightest Light We Have.'"

Bibliography

Ahmed, Sara. *The Cultural Politics of Emotion*. Edinburgh University Press, 2014.

Ahmed, Sara. "Happy Objects." In *The Affect Theory Reader*, edited by Melissa Gregg and Gregory J. Seigworth. Duke University Press, 2010.

Ahn, Heejeh. *Mangseorineun sarang: keipap aidol nollangwa maehogui gongnonjang* [Hesitating love: K-pop idol controversies and the public sphere of fascination]. Owolui bom, 2023.

Ahn, Patty, Michelle Cho, Vernadette Vicuña Gonzalez, Rani Neutill, Mimi Thi Nguyen, and Yutian Wong, eds. *Bangtan Remixed: A Critical BTS Reader*. Duke University Press, 2024.

Aoyagi, Hiroshi. *Islands of Eight Million Smiles: Idol Performance and Symbolic Production in Contemporary Japan*. Harvard University Press, 2005.

Atis, Allison Anne Gray, Noel Sajid I. Murad, and Hannah Ruth L. Sison. "From Purple to Pink: The Filipino ARMY for Leni and the Fight for Good Governance." In Ahn et al., *Bangtan Remixed*.

Baruch, Felicitas. "Transnational Fandom: Creating Alternative Values and New Identities Through Digital Labor." *Television & New Media* 22, no. 6 (2021): 687–702. https://doi.org/10.1177/1527476419898553

Baudinette, Thomas. "Idol Shipping Culture: Exploring Queer Sexuality among Fans of K-Pop." In *The Cambridge Companion to K-Pop*, edited by Suk-Young Kim. Cambridge University Press, 2023.

Baudinette, Thomas. "Sharing Intimacies: Social Media, GMM Fan Events, and BL Idol Fandom." Chap. 4 in *Boys Love Media in Thailand: Celebrity, Fans, and Transnational Asian Queer Popular Culture*. Bloomsbury, 2024.

Benjamin, Jeff. "Classic K-Pop Boy Band SECHSKIES Make Billboard Chart Debut After 20 Years." *Billboard*. May 10, 2017. https://www.billboard.com/articles/columns/k-town/7792162/sechskies-20th-anniversary-world-album-billboard-chart-debut

Berbiguier, Mathieu, and Younghan Cho. "Keipabui hanguk paendeome daehan yeongu: haeoe paendeure daehan insigeul jungsimeuro" [Understanding the Korean Fandom of K-Pop: Focusing on its Perspectives on Foreign Fans]. *Korean Journal of Communication & Information* 81 (2017): 272–98. http://doi.org/10.46407/kjci.2017.02.81.272

Bicker, Laura. "Gangnam: The Scandal Rocking the Playground of K-Pop." *BBC*. June 25, 2019. https://www.bbc.com/news/world-asia-48702763

Bonfils, Michael. "Search Marketing Guide to Naver, Korea's Most Popular Search Engine." *Search Engine Watch*. May 11, 2011. https://www.searchenginewatch.com/2011/05/11/search-marketing-guide-to-naver-koreas-most-popular-search-engine/

Brown, August. "K-Pop's Innocent Image Is Shattered by the 'Burning Sun' Scandal." *Los Angeles Times*. April 5, 2019. https://www.latimes.com/entertainment/music/la-et-ms-burning-sun-20190319-story.html

Chang, WoongJo, and Shin-Eui Park. "The Fandom of Hallyu, a Tribe in the Digital Network Era: The Case of ARMY of BTS." *Kritika Kultura* 32 (2018): 260–87.

Cho, Michelle. "3 Ways That BTS and Its Fans Are Redefining Liveness." *Flow* 24, no. 8 (2018): http://www.flowjournal.org/2018/05/bts-and-its-fans/

Choe, Hun-min. "Gangseonghun aein oppa 'nae myeongui billyeo paenkeulleop huniwoldeu unyeongsa charyeotda'" [Kang Sung Hoon's lover's brother, "He founded the fan club Hoony World under my name"]. *Ilyosinmun*. January 28, 2019. http://ilyo.co.kr/?ac=article_view&entry_id=323745

Choe, Ji-eun. "2016yeonui aidol paendeom" [Idol fandom of 2016]. *IZE*. December 13, 2016. http://ize.co.kr/articleView.html?no=2016121210277283952

Choe, Seon-yun. "Eumwon aep choegangja mellon . . . 3wol iyongja 569manmyeong" [Melon, the strongest music app . . . 5.69 million users in March]. *Newsis*. April 17, 2018. https://mobile.newsis.com/view.html?ar_id=NISX20180417_0000283612#_PA

Choi, JungBong, and Roald Maliangkay, eds. *K-Pop: The International Rise of the Korean Music Industry*. Routledge, 2015.

Choi, Stephanie. "Chart Manipulation and Fan Labor in the Online Moral Economy of K-Pop." In *Introducing Korean Popular Culture*, edited by Youna Kim. Routledge, 2023.

Choi, Stephanie. "K-Pop Idols: Media Commodities, Affective Laborers, and Cultural Capitalists." In *The Cambridge Companion to K-Pop* edited by Suk-Young Kim. Cambridge University Press, 2023.

Chu, Yi Wen. "Poseuteu korona keipap aidol paendeurui gamjeong jageobe gwanhan yeongu: yeongsangtonghwa paen sainhoereul jungsimeuro" [Emotional Work of K-Pop Idol Fans in the Post-Corona Era: Focusing on Video Call Event]. MA thesis, Yonsei University, 2021.

Chung, Siyoung, and Hichang Cho. "Fostering Parasocial Relationships with Celebrities on Social Media: Implications for Celebrity Endorsement." *Psychology & Marketing* 34, no. 4 (2017): 481–95. https://doi.org/10.1002/mar.21001

Click, Melissa A., ed. *Anti-Fandom: Dislike and Hate in the Digital Age*. New York University Press, 2019.

Conquergood, Dwight. "Rethinking Ethnography: Towards a Critical Cultural Politics." *Communication Monographs* 58, no. 2 (1991): 179–94. https://doi.org/10.1080/03637759109376222

Deobeulyuar. *Bangtansonyeondan anpadeon gwageoui na jonna bulssanghada* [How fucking unfortunate I was when I didn't stan BTS]. 2019.

Dong, Sun-hwa. "NCT Member Lucas Goes on Hiatus Following Gaslighting, Cheating Scandal." *Korea Times*. August 26, 2021. https://www.koreatimes.co.kr/www/art/2021/08/732_314537.html

Epstein, Stephen, and James Turnbull. "Girls' Generation? Gender, (Dis)Empowerment, and K-Pop." In *The Korean Popular Culture Reader*, edited by Kyung Hyun Kim and Youngmin Choe. Duke University Press, 2014.

Fedorenko, Olga. "Idol Ads in the Seoul Metro: K-Pop Fandom, Appropriation of Subway Space, and the Right to the City." *City & Society* 33, no. 3 (2021): 492–517. https://doi.org/10.1111/ciso.12415

Galbraith, Patrick W. "'Idols' in Japan, Asia and the World." In *Routledge Handbook of Celebrity Studies*, edited by Anthony Elliott. Routledge, 2018.

Galbraith, Patrick, and Jason G. Karlin, eds. *Idols and Celebrity in Japanese Media Culture*. Palgrave Macmillan, 2012.

Gang, Gyeong-yun. "Gangseonghun, daeman konseoteu chwiso" [Kang Sung Hoon cancels concert in Taiwan]. *SBS*. September 11, 2018. http://sbsfune.sbs.co.kr/news/news_content.jsp?article_id=E10009205184

Gang, Gyeong-yun. "Gangseonghun gosohan paendeul . . . 'jeohuiga wae gangseonghuneul gosohaetnyagoyo?'" [Fans who sued Kang Sung Hoon . . . "Why did we sue Kang Sung Hoon?"]. *SBS*. November 13, 2018. http://sbsfune.sbs.co.kr/news/news_content.jsp?article_id=E10009273132

Gang, Gyeong-yun. "Gangseonghun paendeul, haemyeongyoguseo balpyo . . . 'haemyeongsagwa mothamyeon taltoehara'" [Kang Sung Hoon fans issue a request for explanation . . . "If you can't explain or apologize, leave the group"]. *SBS*. September 20, 2018. http://sbsfune.sbs.co.kr/news/news_content.jsp?article_id=E10009216291

Gang, Yu-mi. "[ASMR] VIDEOCALL with yeongtongpaenssa hugi." YouTube. January 21, 2021. https://www.youtube.com/watch?v=byHbe9g1tLE&t=12s

Gim, Hyeong-chan. "Gimhyeongchanui daejungeumak iyagi <26> namjin nahuna sukmyeongui raibeol" [Gim Hyeong-chan's popular music story <26> Destined Rivals Nam Jin and Na Huna]. *Kookje shinmun*. July 18, 2016. https://www.kookje.co.kr/news2011/asp/newsbody.asp?code=0500&key=20160719.22023183358

Gim, So-yeon. "'YG, jekki jaejeongbi ipjang pyomyeonghara' . . . DCgaelleoli, jipdanhaengdong yego" ["YG, express your position on SECHSKIES' reorganization" . . . DC gallery alerts collective action]. *Hangukgyeongjesinmun*. December 7, 2018. http://news.hankyung.com/article/201812074067H

Gim, Tae-won. "'Daeman paenmiting sagi piso' gangseonghun cheuk, imyeongyeyakseokkaji jakseonghaetda" ["Taiwan fan meeting fraud accused" Kang Sung Hoon even wrote a separate contract]. *Ilyosinmun*. September 17, 2018. http://ilyo.co.kr/?ac=article_view&entry_id=310253

Gim, Tae-won. "Deung dollin paendeom 'gangseonghun taltoehaji aneumyeon konseoteu boikot' choyuui satae" [Fandom turns its back on Kang Sung Hoon, "will boycott concert if he does not leave group"]. *Ilyosinmun*. September 13, 2018. http://ilyo.co.kr/?ac=article_view&entry_id=309675

Gim, Tae-won. "Gangseonghun, daeman paenmiting gwallyeon YG doyong munje bulgeojyeo . . . YG sanghwang paak jung" [Kang Sung Hoon, issue of illegally using YG related to Taiwan fan meeting comes to light . . . YG looking into the situation]. *Ilyosinmun*. September 18, 2018. http://ilyo.co.kr/?ac=article_view&entry_id=310377

Gim, Tae-won. "Hae neomgineun gangseonghun 'ipjang balpyo' . . . YGneun wae chimmukhago itna" [Kang Sung Hoon's "position announcement" as the year passes . . . why is YG silent?]. *Ilyosinmun*. December 12, 2018. http://ilyo.co.kr/?ac=article_view&entry_id=319235

Groszman, Rivkah. "Revisiting Parasocial Theory in Fan Studies: Pathological or (Path) illogical?" *Transformative Works and Cultures* 34 (2020): https://doi.org/10.3983/twc.2020.1989

Han, Jane. "Stars' Fans Become Smart Shareholders." *Korea Times*. April 16, 2018. http://www.koreatimes.co.kr/www/news/biz/2010/05/123_22604.html

Han, Su-jin. "Gangseonghun paenkeulleop Assi, gouiseong yeobue ttara hoengryeong-joe doel sudo" [Kang Sung Hoon fan club's A could be charged with embezzlement depending on whether it was intentional or no]. *The Herald Business*. September 11, 2018. http://biz.heraldcorp.com/culture/view.php?ud=201809111204419716707_1

Hardt, Michael, and Negri, Antonio. *Multitude: War and Democracy in the Age of Empire*. Penguin, 2004.

Herman, Tamar. "Big Hit Entertainment Credits BTS's Success in 2018 to Diverse Fandom and Streaming Culture." *Forbes*. January 29, 2019. https://www.forbes.com/sites/tamarherman/2019/01/29/big-hit-entertainment-credits-bts-success-in-2018-to-diverse-fandom-streaming-culture/?sh=5f23e2401e88

Herman, Tamar. "Blackpink Fans Protest YG Entertainment, Alleging Lack of Promoting Act." *Billboard*. December 16, 2019. https://www.billboard.com/music/music-news/blackpink-fans-protest-yg-entertainment-8546381/

Herman, Tamar. "The Communality of K-Pop Lightsticks." *Notes on K-Pop*. November 14, 2022. https://notesonkpop.com/the-communality-of-k-pop-lightsticks/

Herman, Tamar. "K-Pop Fan Meet-Ups in Hong Kong: Followers of BTS, NCT Dream, Got7 and Others Celebrate Idols' Birthdays, Albums, and More at City Cafes." *South China Morning Post*. April 21, 2021. https://www.scmp.com/lifestyle/k-pop/article/3128933/k-pop-fan-meet-ups-hong-kong-followers-bts-nct-dream-got7-and

Herman, Tamar. "The Unpaid Labor of K-Pop Fan Translation Twitter." *Forbes*. August 20, 2020. https://www.forbes.com/sites/tamarherman/2020/08/20/the-unpaid-labor-of-k-pop-fan-translation-twitter/

Hills, Matt. "Returning to 'Becoming-a-Fan' Stories: Theorising Transformational Objects and the Emergence/Extension of Fandom," In *The Ashgate Research Companion to Fan Cultures*, edited by Linda Duits, Koos Zwaan, and Stijn Reijnders. Ashgate, 2014.

Hinck, Ashley. "Ethical Frameworks and Ethical Modalities: Theorizing Communication and Citizenship in a Fluid World." *Communication Theory* 26, no. 1 (2016): 1–20. https://doi.org/10.1111/comt.12062

Horton, David, and Richard Wohl. "Mass Communication and Para-Social Interaction: Observation on Intimacy at a Distance." *Psychiatry* 19, no. 3 (1956): 215–29.

Inkigayo. SBS. https://programs.sbs.co.kr/enter/gayo/main

Jang, Jin-ri. "YG cheuk 'gangseonghungwa jeonsokgyeyak haeji, apeurodo jal doegil baranda'" [YG, "We have terminated our exclusive contract with Kang Sung Hoon and wish him well"]. *OSEN*. January 1, 2019. https://entertain.naver.com/read?oid=109&aid=0003929775

Jenkins, Henry. *Textual Poachers: Television Fans and Participatory Culture*. Routledge, 1992.

Jenkins, Henry, and Sangita Shresthova. "Up, up, and away! The Power and Potential of Fan Activism." *Transformative Works and Cultures* 10 (2012): https://doi.org/10.3983/twc.2012.0435

Jeong, Areum. "How the Pyŏnsa Stole the Show: The Performance of the Korean Silent Film Narrators." *Media Convergence Research* 25 (2018): 25–60. https://doi.org/10.22814/sgjcr.2018..25.25

Jeong, Areum. "K-Pop: Stream Like You Breathe" *Korea Exposé*. November 28, 2017. https://www.koreaexpose.com/K-pop-stream-breathe/

Jin, Dal Yong, and Kyoung Yoon. "The Social Mediascape of Korean Pop Culture: Hallyu 2.0 as Spreadable Media Practice." *New Media & Society* 18, no. 7 (2016): 1,277–92. https://doi.org/10.1177/1461444814554895

Jung, Min-Woo, and Na-Young Lee. "Fandom Managing Stars, Entertainment Industry Managing Fandom." *Media, Gender, & Culture* 12 (2009): 191–240. https://www.dbpia.co.kr/journal/articleDetail?nodeId=NODE01278477

Jung, Sun. "K-Pop, Indonesian Fandom, and Social Media." *Transformative Works and Cultures* 8 (2011): http://dx.doi.org/10.3983/twc.2011.0289

Kang, Bora, Jihee Seo, and Sunhee Kim. "20dae yeoseong paendeomui gamjeong gujowa munhwa silcheon: <peurodyuseu 101 sijeun 2> paendeomeul jungsimeuro" [The Affective Structure and Cultural Practice of Fandom: Women Fandom in Their 20s: Focus on *Produce 101, Season 2* Fandom]. *Media, Gender & Culture* 33, no. 1 (2018): 5–50. https://doi.org/10.38196/mgc.2018.03.33.1.5

Kang, Eunkyo. "Aelbeomkkangui gippeumgwa seulpeum" [The ups and downs of album unboxing]. *Design* 536 (2023): 92–93.

Kang, Eunkyo. "Keipab aidorui japil sagwamun: songeulssiui jinjeongseonggwa paendeomui sobija jeongcheseong" [Handwritten Apologies of K-Pop Idols: Authenticity of Handwriting and Fandom's Identity as Consumer]. *Feminism and Korean Literature* 51 (2020): 36–71. https://doi.org/10.15686/fkl.2020..51.36

Kang, Eunkyo. "Yeonghwa *Seongdeok* daedam 3 gibuhago yeoronjeoneul pyeolchineun jeongchijeok jonjaero jinhwahae on" [Film *Seongdeok* interview 3 evolving into a political entity that donates and wages a war of public opinion]. *Cine 21*. September 30, 2022. http://m.cine21.com/news/view/?mag_id=101001

Kang, Shin-kyu, and Jun Hyung Lee. "Saengsangwa sobi sai, noriwa nodong sai: <peurodyuseu 48>gwa paendeomui jaeguseong [Between Producing and Consuming, Playing and Laboring: Reconstruction of <Produce 48> and Fandom]. *Korean Journal of Journalism & Communication Studies* 63, no. 5 (2019): 269–315. https://www.dbpia.co.kr/journal/articleDetail?nodeId=NODE09226197

Keskin, Alptekin, and Mutlu Binark. "Yoongi, Can You Hear Me?: Demanding Justice for #Melisa and ARMY Activism in Turkey." In Ahn et al., *Bangtan Remixed*.

Kim, Eunjung. "Nyumidieo sidaeui paendeomgwa munhwamaegaeja: bangtansonyeondan saryereul jungsimeuro" [Fandom and New Cultural Intermediary in New Media Era: Focusing on the Case of BTS]. *Journal of the Korea Contents Association* 20, no. 1 (2020): 378–91. https://doi.org/10.5392/JKCA.2020.20.01.378

Kim, Gooyong. *From Factory Girls to K-Pop Idol Girls: Cultural Politics of Developmentalism, Patriarchy, and Neoliberalism in South Korea's Popular Music Industry*. Lexington Books, 2019.

Kim, Ji, Mick Shin, and Jane Do. *Bumping into BTS*. Jikim Publishing, 2020.

Kim, Jungwon. *Eumagillyuhakjaui keipapagi: daejungeumak, paendeom, geurigo jeongcheseong [Ethnomusicologist's K-Popping: Popular Music, Fandom, and Identities]*. Sechang Publishing, 2022.

Kim, Jungwon. "Home and Homma in K-Pop Fandom: From Fan Sites and Paparazzi to

Black Market and Cultural Producers." *Journal of Korea Culture Industry* 18, no. 3 (2018): 1–10. https://doi.org/10.35174/JKCI.2018.09.18.3.1

Kim, Jungwon. "'With the Brightest Light We Have': K-Pop Fandom in Candlelight Movement and Diversification of Korean Protest Culture." In *The Candlelight Movement, Democracy, and Communication in Korea*, edited by JongHwa Lee, Chuyun Oh, and Yong-Chan Kim. Routledge, 2022.

Kim, Seongcheol, and Dal Yong Jin. *Korea's Platform Empire: An Emerging Power in the Global Platform Sphere*. Routledge, 2024.

Kim, Sooah. "Aidol yukseong peurogeuraem, aidol geurubui 'gongjeonghan' seonbareul wihan moheom" [Idol Fostering Program: An Adventure for 'Fair' Selection of Idol Groups]. *Culture Science* 92 (2017): 285–98. https://www.dbpia.co.kr/journal/articleDetail?nodeId=NODE07293776

Kim, Sooah. "Sosyeol wep sidae paendeom munhwaui byeonhwa" [The Dynamics of Fandom in the Age of Social Media]. *Journal of Cybercommunication Academic Society* 31, no. 1 (2014): 45–94. https://www.dbpia.co.kr/journal/articleDetail?nodeId=NODE02380847

Kim, Sujeong. "Paendeomgwa peminijeumui jou: peminijeum gwanjeomeseo bon paendeom yeonguui seonggwawa jaengjeom" [When Fandom Meets Feminism—Issues and Achievements of Fandom Studies from a Feminism Perspective]. *Journal of Communication Research* 55, no. 3 (2018): 47–86. https://www.dbpia.co.kr/journal/articleDetail?nodeId=NODE07519831

Kim, Sujeong, and Sooah Kim. "Haedok paereodaimeul neomeo suhaeng paereodaimeuro: paendeom yeonguui hyeonhwanggwa jaengjeom" [From Interpretation Paradigm to Performance Paradigm]. *Korean Journal of Broadcasting and Telecommunication Studies* 29, no. 4 (2015): 33–81. https://www.dbpia.co.kr/journal/articleDetail?nodeId=NODE06397135

Kim, Sujeong, and Sooah Kim. "Jipdanjeok dodeokjuui etoseu: honjongjeok keipabui hangukjeok munhwajeongcheseong" [The Ethos of Collective Moralism: The Korean Cultural Identity of K-Pop]. *Media & Society* 23, no. 3 (2015): 5–52. https://www.dbpia.co.kr/journal/articleDetail?nodeId=NODE06507953

Kim, Suk-Young. *K-Pop Live: Fans, Idols, and Multimedia Performance*. Stanford University Press, 2018.

Kim, Victoria. "K-Pop's K-Porn Problem: Growing Scandal Highlights South Korea's Spy-Cam Epidemic." *Los Angeles Times*. April 3, 2019. https://www.latimes.com/world/asia/la-fg-kpop-porn-scandal-20190403-story.html

Kim, Youna. "Introduction: Korean Media in a Digital Cosmopolitan World." In *The Korean Wave: Korean Media Go Global*, edited by Youna Kim. Routledge, 2013.

King-O'Riain, Rebecca Chiyoko. "'They Were Having So Much Fun, So Genuinely . . .': K-Pop Fan Online Affect and Corroborated Authenticity." *New Media & Society* 23, no. 9 (2020): 1–19. https://doi.org/10.1177/1461444820941194

Ko, Hyeri, and Eunkyung Yang. "Namseong aidol geurubui yeoseonghyeomo nollangwa yeoseong paendeomui bunyeol" [Korean Boy Group's Misogyny and Division Between Female Fandom]. *Journal of the Korea Contents Association* 17, no. 8 (2017): 506–19. https://www.dbpia.co.kr/journal/articleDetail?nodeId=NODE07230115

Kompare, Derek. "Fan Curators and Gateways into Fandom." In *The Routledge Companion to Media Fandom*, edited by Melissa A. Click and Suzanne Scott. Routledge, 2018.

Koskinen, Kaisa. *Translation and Affect: Essays on Sticky Affects and Translational Affective Labour*. John Benjamins Publishing, 2020.

Kowert, Rachel, and Emory Daniel Jr. "The One-and-a-Half Sided Parasocial Relationship: The Curious Case of Live Streaming." *Computers in Human Behavior Reports* 4 (2021): 1–7. https://doi.org/10.1016/j.chbr.2021.100150

Kpop4planet. https://www.kpop4planet.com/.

Kwon, Jungmin. *Straight Korean Female Fans and Their Gay Fantasies*. University of Iowa Press, 2019.

Laffan, Derek A. "Positive Psychosocial Outcomes and Fanship in K-Pop Fans: A Social Identity Theory Perspective." *Psychological Reports* 124, no. 5 (2020): 1–14. https://doi.org/10.1177/0033294120961524

Lee, Gyu Tag. "Keipabui segyehwawa dijiteolhwa—yutubeu baneung dongyeongsang-gwa keobeodaenseu gyeongyeondaehoe" [Digitalization and Globalization of K-Pop—YouTube Reaction Video & Cover Dance Festival]. *Journal of Hallyu Business* 1, no. 1 (2014): 73–107. https://kiss.kstudy.com/Detail/Ar?key=3322556

Lee, Heejoo. *Hwansangtong* [Phantom Pain]. Munhakdongne. 2016.

Lee, Hun-Yul, and Hye Min Ji. "Paendeom naeui gyecheung gubyeore daehan yeongu: teuwiteowa paen saengsanjareul jungsimero" [A Study on Discrimination Inside Fandom in Korea—Focusing on Fan Producers in Twitter Activities]*Media, Gender & Culture* 30, no. 4 (2015): 5–40. https://www.dbpia.co.kr/journal/articleDetail?nodeId=NODE06577061

Lee, Naeun. "Chinmilhwansangui jakdong bangsik: paenpeullaetpom 'beobeul' iyongjareul jungsimeuro" [How the Intimacy Fantasy Works: Focusing on the Fan Platform 'Bubble' Users]. *Media, Gender & Culture* 37, no. 2 (2022): 157–254. https://doi.org/10.38196/mgc.2022.06.37.2.157

Lee, Seung-Ah. "Of the Fans, by the Fans, for the Fans." In *Hallyu 2.0: The Korean Wave in the Age of Social Media*, edited by Sangjoon Lee and Abe Mark Nornes. University of Michigan Press, 2015.

Lee, Wonseok, and Grace Kao. "'I Need U': Audience Participation in BTS's Online Concerts During COVID-19." *Journal of Popular Music Studies* 35, no. 1 (2023): 46–66. https://doi.org/10.1525/jpms.2023.35.1.46

Lee, Wonseok, and Grace Kao. "'Make It Right': Why #BlackLivesMatter(s) to K-Pop, BTS, and BTS ARMYs." *IASPM Journal* 11, no. 1 (2021): 70–87. https://iaspmjournal.net/index.php/IASPM_Journal/article/view/1113

Lie, Jae-Won. "Sosyeol midieo sahoeyeongyeolseongui paendeom gongdongche hyeong-seonge gwanhan tamsaekjeok yeongu: bangtansonyeondan saryereul jungsimero" [How Does the Social Connectivity of Social Media Build a Fandom Community? An Exploratory Study on the BTS Fandom]. *Journal of the Korea Contents Association* 21, no. 7 (2021): 1–12. http://doi.org/10.5392/JKCA.2021.21.07.001

Lopez, Lori Kido. "Fan-Activists and the Politics of Race in *The Last Airbender*." *International Journal of Cultural Studies* 15, no. 5 (2012): 1–15. https://doi.org/10.1177/1367877911422862

Mabokpil. YouTube. https://www.youtube.com/channel/UC7MQxkON_yXQjJv60hBIW1w/featured

Madison, D. Soyini. *Acts of Activism: Human Rights as Radical Performance*. Cambridge University Press, 2010.

Maguncia, Jeremiah Estela. "OMG! Reaction Videos on YouTube: Meanings to Fandom and to K-Pop Community." MA thesis, Seoul National University, 2014.

McLaren, Courtney, and Dal Yong Jin. "You Can't Help But Love Them: BTS, Transcultural Fandom, and Affective Identities." *Korea Journal* 60, no. 1 (2020): 100–127. https://doi.org/10.25024/kj.2020.60.1.100

M Countdown. Mnet. https://www.mnetplus.world/community/main?communityId=PzfktaFfF9GXMF1CBSnUO

Music Bank. KBS. [*Mujikbaengkeu*.] https://program.kbs.co.kr/2tv/enter/musicbank/pc/index.html

No, Jin-ho. "Aidol paendeul nalbam saeumyeo 'eumwon jibungkik' . . . chateu 1wi jeonjaeng" [Idol fans stay up all night and "kick the roof of the music charts" . . . battle for the top spot on the charts]. *The Joongang*. March 8, 2017. https://www.joongang.co.kr/article/21348101#home

O, Se-yeon (Seyeon Oh). *Seongdeok* [*Fanatic*]. Film. 2021.

Octaviany, Karlina. "Break the Structure: BTS ARMY Digital Activism and State Surveillance in Indonesia's Omnibus Law Protest." In Ahn et al., *Bangtan Remixed*.

Oh, Chuyun. "From Seoul to Copenhagen: Migrating K-Pop Cover Dance and Performing Diasporic Youth in Social Media." *Dance Research Journal* 52, no. 1 (2020): 20–32. https://doi.org/10.1017/S0149767720000030

Oh, Chuyun. "Queering Spectatorship in K-Pop: The Androgynous Male Dancing Body and Western Female Fandom." *Journal of Fandom Studies* 3, no.1 (2015): 59–78. https://doi.org/10.1386/jfs.3.1.59_1

Oh, Chuyun, and David C. Oh. "White-Expat-Fans' Performing K-Pop Other on YouTube." *Text and Performance Quarterly* 42, no.2 (2022): 198–219. https://doi.org/10.1080/10462937.2022.2062441

Oh, David C. "Black K-Pop Fan Videos and Polyculturalism." *Popular Communication* 15, no. 4 (2017): 269–82. https://doi.org/10.1080/15405702.2017.1371309

Oh, David. "Korean Wave| K-Pop Fans React: Hybridity and the White Celebrity-Fan on YouTube." *International Journal of Communication* 11 (2017): 18. https://ijoc.org/index.php/ijoc/article/view/6307

Oh, Heera. *Gwamorip deokhureul wihan taldeok annaeseo* [Exit guide for deeply immersed fans]. 2021. https://brunch.co.kr/brunchbook/nanafan.

Oh, Heera. *Naneun naui paeni doellaeyo: gwamorip deokhureul wihan taldeok annaeseo* [I want to be a fan of myself: Exit guide for deeply immersed fans]. 2020.

Oh, Youjeong. "Following the Footsteps of BTS: The Global Rise of K-Pop Tourism." In *The Cambridge Companion to K-Pop* edited by Suk-Young Kim. Cambridge University Press, 2023.

Oh, Youjeong. *Pop City: Korean Popular Culture and the Selling of Place*. Cornell University Press, 2018.

Puzar, Aljosa, and Yewon Hong. "Korean Cuties: Understanding Performed Winsomeness (*Aegyo*) in South Korea." *Asia Pacific Journal of Anthropology* 19, no. 4 (2018): 333–349. https://doi.org/10.1080/14442213.2018.1477826

Saeji, CedarBough T. "Making Icons: The Rise of the K-Pop Adjacent Industries." *Inter-Asia Cultural Studies* (July 2024): 1–22. https://doi.org/10.1080/14649373.2024.2365594

Saeji, CedarBough T. "The Seungri Scandal and South Korea's Gender Disparity." *Korea Exposé*. April 13, 2019. https://www.koreaexpose.com/what-seungri-burning-sun-scandal-says-about-korea-gender-disparity/

Shin, Layoung. "Queer Eye for K-Pop Fandom: Popular Culture, Cross-Gender Performance, and Queer Desire in South Korean Cosplay of K-Pop Stars." *Korea Journal* 58, no. 4 (2018): 87–113. https://www.dbpia.co.kr/journal/articleDetail?nodeId=NODE09378596

The Show. SBS Medianet. https://programs.sbs.co.kr/sbsm/theshow/main

Show Champion. MBC PLUS. https://m.mbcplus.com/web/program/contentList.do?programInfoSeq=67

Show! Music Core. [*Syo! eumakjungsim*.] MBC. https://program.imbc.com/musiccore

Son, Elizabeth W. *Embodied Reckonings: "Comfort Women," Performance, and Transpacific Redress*. University Michigan Press, 2018.

Springman, Laura. "'It's Army Versus the U.S. Army': K-Pop Fans, Activism, and #BlackLivesMatter," *Flow* 26, no. 10 (2020). https://www.flowjournal.org/2020/08/its-army-versus-the-army/

Stanfill, Mel, and Megan Condis. "Fandom and/as Labor." *Transformative Works and Cultures* 15 (2014). https://doi.org/10.3983/twc.2014.0593

Sun, Meicheng. "K-Pop Fan Labor and an Alternative Creative Industry: A Case Study of GOT7 Chinese Fans." *Global Media and China* 5, no. 4 (2020): 389–406. https://doi.org/10.1177/2059436420954588

Swan, Anna Lee. "Transnational Identities and Feeling in Fandom: Place and Embodiment in K-Pop Fan Reaction Videos." *Communication, Culture and Critique* 11, no. 4 (2018): 548–65. https://doi.org/10.1093/ccc/tcy026.

Team Nunaz. *Oneurui halil: bangtan* [To do list: BTS]. 2020.

"V-LIVE—Star Live App." Google Play. 2018. https://play.google.com/store/apps/details?id=com.naver.vapp.

Yeo, Hyeon-gu. "Akpeulleo gonggyeoge jekseukiseu paendeuri naseo daesin haenaen il [What SECHSKIES fans did in response to malicious commenters]." *The JoongAng*. September 15, 2017. https://www.joongang.co.kr/article/21939170#home

Yi, Yu-jin. "Haibu, aidol paensainhoeseo sogotgeomsa" [HYBE checks underwear at idol fansign]. *Hankyoreh*. July 10, 2023. https://www.hani.co.kr/arti/society/society_general/1099421.html

Yi, Yu-na. "Bangtansonyeondan 'yeohyeom nollan gasa, simnyeokkichyeo joesong' gongsiksagwa [sagwamun jeonmun]" [BTS issues official apology, "We apologize for causing any inconvenience due to controversial lyrics about misogyny" {Full apology letter}]. *Chosun ilbo*. July 6, 2016. https://www.chosun.com/site/data/html_dir/2016/07/06/2016070602522.html

Yim, Hui-yoon. "'Bangtansonyeondan oppadeul, yeohyeomieyo?' . . . ilbu paen, gasateuwiteo geul haemyeong yogu" ["BTS oppas, are you hating on women?" Some fans demand clarification of lyrics and Twitter posts]. *Donga ilbo*. July 6, 2016. https://www.donga.com/news/Culture/article/all/20160706/79039096/1

Yudeokmo. "Press conference of a retiring Lucas stan ft. Bubble msgs." YouTube. September 1, 2021. https://www.youtube.com/watch?v=gekPZAtqqfg

Yun Su-jeong. "Nahuna jechigo badeun 3nyeon yeonsok gasuwang sangpae 'oppa ajik saraitda'" [Recipient of best singer award and beats Na Huna 3 years in a row, "I still got it"]. *Chosun ilbo*. October 10, 2023. https://www.chosun.com/culture-life/culture_general/2023/10/10/GFD7K25BOZBODOZEPEDGIDTQJU/

Yun, Yeo-il. *Modeun hyeonjaeui sijak, 1990nyeondae* [The beginning of everything present, the 1990s]. Dolbaegae, 2023.

Zhang, Qian, and Keith Negus. "East Asian Pop Music Idol Production and the Emergence of Data Fandom in China." *International Journal of Cultural Studies* 23, no. 4 (2020): 1–19. https://doi.org/10.1177/1367877920904064

Zhong, Wenfang. "Hommaui paendeom saengsanhwaldongeul tonghaeseo jomyeong-han hommaui yeokalgwa nodongui munhwajeok hamui" [Study on the Cultural Implications of Homema's Role and Labor by Illuminating the Homema's Production Activities in Fandom]. MA thesis, Kyung Hee University, 2020.

Index

Italicized page numbers refer to photographs.